Shadow Mothers

Shadow Mothers
STORIES OF ADOPTION AND REUNION

Linda Back McKay

NORTH STAR PRESS OF ST. CLOUD, INC.

This book is dedicated
to David and Abbot
for their wisdom and patience.

Certain names in these stories have been changed to protect the privacy of the individuals.

Cover art: John Stevens, Daytona Beach, Florida.

Copyright © 1998 Linda Back McKay

All Rights Reserved. No part of this book may be used or reproduced in any manner without written permission of the publisher, except in the case of brief quotations in literary articles and reviews.

Printed in the United States of America by Versa Press, Inc., East Peoria, IL.

Published by: North Star Press of St. Cloud, Inc.
                 P.O. Box 451
                 St. Cloud, Minnesota 56302

Foreword

Mother's Day, 1998. My son and his wife are going to make me a grand-mother again. This is a priceless gift. Another gift that was never expected. Does it make up for losing him at babyhood? Does finding him make up for twenty years of not knowing?

I was born whole, then spent some years disintegrating. I lived with it. I built myself again, not without risk, but with a soft voice for babies. I was valiant. I survived. I decided to be happy. I built a whole family.

I went on, because it is what people do. Raised the other children I could have. I swallowed the experience, and it became my blood and bones. Every-thing I lived was taken inside me like food—bitter and sweet—to rest in quiet inside places. The loss is eternal and settles into another set of wrinkles across my forehead. I am not angry anymore. A little sad, yes, and humbly grateful at the same time. I put the sad in a box in the back of a high shelf.

What I have lived is almost obsolete. It is a recipe not for sharing. The ingredients are rare, and that is good. That recipe for dragon stew should be wrapped in white linen and placed in an attic chest. It should molder in the dry heat of history.

*   *   *

Acknowledgments

Heartfelt thanks to Barbara Leigh Kaplan who embarked on this journey with me.

Warm wishes also to the women who entrusted their stories to us. This is your book, and you are instrumental in whatever positive results may grow from it.

Thanks to Judith Connor for her friendship and artistry. And to Amy Dietz Haggenmiller and Holly Fields for their copy editing assistance.

A loving thank you to my family, Becka Mara, Michele, Joel, Katie Zin, Tom, and Becky, for understanding the need to write this book. Love also to Allie Rose, who doesn't appear here, except as a dream.

The poem, "Dance with Dad," was first published in *Those Girls Are Always Dancing* (1996, White Space Press). Linda Back McKay wishes to thank the editors of *Lipservice, Minnesota Monthly, Parting Gifts* and *The Antigonish Review,* the publications in which some of the other poems included here first appeared.

The song lyrics from "Super-Human," "Unconventional," "Bad Love," "Just Can't Leave Your Love," "Years in the Future," and "Angel" are the property of Jan Seides-Murphy, all rights reserved.

Introduction

Behind the sensational headlines, celebrity talk shows, and tabloid perceptions lie the secrets and truths of real women who each placed a child for adoption and years later were reunited. There is much more woven into the tapestry of our lives than the pain of loss and the joy of reunion. Each of our stories has a beginning as well as an afterwards.

The ten women who tell their stories here do not share the same history. We are from various parts of the country with a wide range of social and economic backgrounds. We have only this one experience in common, and it joins our families together in a community of understanding.

Out of the shadows, we come to share the peace and acceptance we have discovered through the telling of our stories. If you are a woman like us, a child like ours, a birth father, one of the parents who made room in your life for a child when we could not, or someone with whom we shared our lives afterwards—you are part of this story, too. We hope our stories help you see why we must tell them.

*   *   *

Contents

Chapter One

๑ *Bonnie* ๛

Our family was Southern through and through— from the depth of our religious convictions to the height of our moral standards. We were Mother, my brother Paul, Daddy, and me. A completely traditional family, we went to church not once but three times a week. Daddy was a Baptist deacon, and both my parents were Sunday school teachers. I liked going to church when I was little because I could get dressed up in one of my many frilly dresses. I was one of the best-dressed girls in town, and I had perfect attendance at Sunday school for seven years. It's true that I came from a good home, but perhaps I was too sheltered and given too much.

We lived in a small town just outside of Atlanta, Georgia, which was not the big city it is today. In the 1950s and 1960s, there were no interstate highways, and a shopping trip into Atlanta was always a big event, full of excitement and anticipation.

Daddy was a railroad conductor. His usual route was between Atlanta and Chattanooga, and he rode the caboose. The tracks were across the road from our house. When his train would come by, I'd shout, "Here comes Daddy's train!" Then we'd all run out to the front porch to wave. I was allowed to ride on the train for free any time I wished. It was so much fun!

Daddy's family were all pillars of the community, but Mother's relations apparently were not. My mother's parents lived with us.

"Papa" was a diabetic with an artificial leg, which fascinated me. He was sort of emotional and would cry sometimes when he talked about his mother. As a young woman, his mother lived in a small shack in the moun-

1

tains of West Virginia and worked hard to raise her five children. She "took sick" and died when Papa was about ten, leaving his father to provide for the family as best he could. Papa was forced to go to work. Because of his early responsibilities, Papa only had a few years of "schooling" and only learned to read a little when he was in the army. He was very embarrassed about this and blamed his lack of education for his lack of job opportunities.

"Mama" had a rough childhood, too. At age eleven she went to work in a textile factory. She was so small that she had to stand on a stool to reach the large spools of thread. Needless to say, this was all before the child labor laws.

Mama liked to "dip" snuff. She always kept a tin can nearby—her "spit can." Her sisters and Papa's brothers all either dipped or chewed tobacco. One weekend when I was about five, my great aunts and great uncles were visiting at our house. This was probably 1954, and playing "Cowboys and Indians" was all the rage. My brother Paul and I wanted to make "Indian arrows," so we sneaked out to the chicken coop to pull feathers from one of our sitting hens. (We let the hens sit on their eggs only when we wanted baby chicks.) I didn't realize it, but on one side of the pen was a huge wasp nest. I popped my head right into it, and before I knew it, I was covered with wasps!

Screaming, I ran to Mama and the rest of the old folks on the porch. Do you know what they did to treat my stings? Spit tobacco juice all over me! I couldn't believe they were doing this! But it worked. Who knows—that home remedy might have saved my life.

Paul and I loved Mama and Papa with all our hearts and souls, and we knew they loved us, too. But Mother told us far-fetched tales about their having been abusive alcoholics. She said that she and her sister were "good girls from a bad home."

According to Mother, Papa would work every day, but then he'd drink from Friday night straight through Sunday. She said Mama drank with him, and they'd have huge fights. Mother said one time Papa even chased Mama around the house shooting a gun! It was hard for us to believe these things, because Mama and Papa were nothing but sweet to us. Anyway, as my grandparents aged, Papa's health problems set in, and they didn't have much money. When they asked Mother if they could live with us, she said they could, as long as there was no alcohol in the house. Nobody ever did bring alcohol into that house. Never.

Daddy (I still call him Daddy) and I have always been very close. I remember sitting on his lap, prattling on about every little thing that had happened to me that day, and him just listening. Smiling, stroking my head and listening. I was his little darling.

I think Mother was jealous of my closeness with Daddy. She liked my brother best, though, and that was obvious to me. She always seemed to have time to talk to Paul, but not me. Mother had health problems and was sick off and on from the time I was a baby. At first, they thought she had cancer, but it was actually some other type of inoperable growth, which made one of her lungs collapse.

With her respiratory and heart problems, Mother couldn't handle house work, but she was able to work as a secretary. She tired easily and was often worn out when she came home at night. I don't remember that she ever had much time or energy to be with me.

I loved and admired Paul, who was eight years older than I. He was very talented musically and extremely popular. I couldn't wait to get older. I remember wishing my childhood would end, so I could go to high school and be just like him.

As luck would have it, I ended up hating high school. In 1963, when I started ninth grade, the Atlanta district lines were changed, and I was separated from most of my friends. Also, the school systems in the South were not exactly the greatest. I was an intelligent kid, and I felt like I was wasting my time in school, having already learned most of what was presented. I started playing hooky a lot and hanging around with older kids—mostly older boys.

As you might expect, sex was not a subject of discussion in my family. It was mostly treated as if it didn't exist, except within the sanctity of marriage. Mother did prepare me for having my period by giving me only the basic facts. One of my most vivid memories about Mother's guidance took place when I was about fourteen. She told me how proud she was to have kept herself "pure," and how wonderful it was on her wedding night to have saved herself for her husband.

When I brought up the subject of premarital sex, Mother said, "I would rather see you dead than pregnant before you get married." Believe me, I have never forgotten that statement.

A horrible thing happened when I was thirteen. I found out that my brother "had" to get married. He didn't tell my parents that his fiancée was pregnant, though. They never knew about it until after the baby was born. They thought my nephew was born early—at six months! But then Paul confessed, and after the initial shock the subject was never mentioned again.

Maybe if I'd been satisfied in school, things might have turned out differently for me, but I guess we'll never know. When I was fifteen, I became romantically involved with B.J., an eighteen-year-old college student. If truth be told, he had been my sweetheart since I was about eleven. We used to meet behind the schoolhouse and kiss, but we didn't actually date until I was fifteen.

I thought myself quite mature, and we eventually started having sex. I felt happy and guilty at the same time. This relationship with "an older man" distanced me from my classmates and made me think of myself as older than they were. When I was sixteen, B.J. became a part-time student with a full-time job. Because this was 1965 and the war in Vietnam was heating up, he was drafted almost immediately. I wanted desperately for him to marry me, but he said I'd have to wait until he got home.

I'm ashamed to admit it now, but I was so angry at him. "What?" I exclaimed. "You want me to wait a whole year to get married? You must be kidding!"

We had a big, ugly fight and broke up. Then he was shipped overseas.

I felt completely alone in the world after B.J. left. Mother and Daddy must have been concerned about me, but I was too involved in my own problems to notice. I didn't feel like a teenager, but I knew I wasn't an adult either. I couldn't relate to the few friends I had.

One night I went to a teen dance with my friends and in walked Jimmy Paulson, the most handsome hunk of man I'd ever seen. I think my heart actually skipped a beat when he asked me to dance. We danced to a few songs and then went out to his car, where we talked and listened to the radio. He had a funny sense of humor and made me feel like I was his equal, even though I was sixteen and he was twenty-two.

Bonnie

For the next year or so we dated—dinner and the movies, most often the drive-in movies—where we petted heavily. Eventually we went "all the way." During this time, he had met my family and even joined us for Sunday dinners. Mother and Daddy approved of him. They never suspected what we were doing. Sometimes I would sneak off to meet him at night when my parents were asleep. We were terribly in love. Everything was great, but all good things must come to an end, right? One night the condom slipped off.

I had assumed that we would marry when I finished high school. Then when I was pretty sure I was pregnant, I thought we would go ahead and marry right away. When I told him I was pregnant he became very sad and apologetic. Tears came to his eyes and he said, "I am so sorry for what I've done to you."

It didn't matter if he was really sorry or not. Turns out, his name wasn't even Jimmy. It was Billy—and he was already married! What's more, his wife was pregnant, too! Our relationship came to a screeching halt.

Looking back on it, I don't want to judge him too harshly. He was hurt by the situation, and after all, a lot of people do things they shouldn't.

But then my whole world felt suddenly blown apart. The man I loved was not even who I thought he was! Everything had been a lie.

I can barely remember anything about the first few months of my pregnancy. I think I was in shock. I didn't know what to do. I had some crazy thoughts. I pretended none of it was true—that everything would go away if I pretended hard enough.

I thought about having an abortion but didn't know where or how to find out about such a thing. I thought I would run away to California where my cousin Annie lived. Maybe she would help me. I even made plane reservations. But my parents somehow found out that I was planning to run away. That's when they confronted me about my "weight gain."

I was five and one-half months along and, of course, would not have approached my mother with the news, given her earlier comment about rather seeing me dead than pregnant. When my parents did find out, such a look of sadness came over Daddy's face. And then he cried. I had not ever seen him cry before. That sad look never went away, and I was never able to look him

5

straight in the eye after that day. I still can't. Mother was near tears, too, and shaking. I remember being afraid she'd have a heart attack, given her already bad health.

But Mother somehow pulled herself together and took the bull by the horns. She had read about maternity homes in a "Dear Abby" column and called the one closest to Atlanta. It was full, and there was a long waiting list. I had no idea there were so many girls who had gotten in trouble! Mother was anxious to get me somewhere where I could get professional help. She and Daddy thought I was near some type of breakdown, and maybe I was.

Another really sad thing happened during this time. My old boyfriend B.J. came back from Vietnam on a thirty-day leave and appeared at our door one day. He said he still cared for me and wondered if we could get back together again! I had to tell him that I was pregnant—with another man's baby. He was devastated. I felt so guilty!

I didn't tell anybody who the father of my baby was. Daddy kept pressuring me to tell him, but I was afraid he would go and kill Billy if he knew what he had done to me.

Mother suddenly became very involved in my life. She was terrified that Daddy's family would find out about my pregnancy, so she concocted a story about my having quit school to accept a job in another town, where I was living in a women's boarding house. She must have been a really good liar because nobody—not even my brother or Mama and Papa—guessed the real story. To them, I had simply gone off on vacation with my parents, found a job and didn't come home for several months. Everybody bought it!

I arrived at the home in Tennessee July 7, 1967, the day after my eighteenth birthday. I was six months pregnant and, with the help of a tight girdle, had successfully hidden my condition from virtually everyone.

I was advised that during my stay I could use either my real first name or an alias, if I preferred. All the girls were instructed never to disclose their last name to anyone. We were also told that if we ever saw any of the girls after we left the home, we were not to acknowledge each other. "After a short length of time," was the official message, "your lives will be back on track and you will forget about this terrible ordeal."

Bonnie

A social worker provided counseling, but no option other than adoption was ever discussed with me. I was not offered any help or advice about how I might manage to keep my baby. I was not advised of my legal rights; nor was I told about the possible long-term emotional consequences of relinquishment.

At the home, if a girl openly expressed a desire to keep her baby, she was forced to leave. I remember one girl who decided to keep her baby after it was born. She was not allowed to return to the home—not even to pick up her belongings.

Those of us remaining received a stern lecture about the awful thing she had done by refusing to sign the adoption papers. Her entire family would be disgraced, and the child would grow up feeling embarrassed and not as good as other children. We were warned never to discuss her situation among ourselves, or we would be in danger of being expelled from the home.

The girls I met at the maternity home were nothing like what I had expected. They were just regular girls, like me. Most of them had been attending college or working as secretaries before this. A few were still in high school. The youngest was fifteen and the oldest twenty-six. There was one black nurse who was being discharged from the army because she became pregnant. All the others were white, middle- and upper-class girls. They were not promiscuous. Many of them had only the one affair with a boyfriend who made a hasty disappearing act upon learning of the pregnancy.

I still think about one particular girl from the home. She had been engaged to marry her baby's father after his tour in Vietnam. He never returned. She gave birth to twins and placed them for adoption. She didn't even tell her fiancé's parents that she was pregnant. I think it is so sad that a couple lost their son in that senseless war and never knew that his twin babies—their grandchildren—were given away to strangers.

When I look back on the birth of my son, I can't believe Mother and Daddy let me go through it completely alone. That was so cruel! Even to this day, it makes me feel like nobody in the world really cared about me. They never even visited me in the hospital after the baby was born. I think the personnel from the home told them not to visit. Maybe if they had seen the baby, they might have encouraged me to keep him.

Shadow Mothers

My labor began late at night. I endured it as long as I could but became very afraid and called the "house mother." She told me to start timing my contractions and to wait until they were five minutes apart before bothering her again. She even asked me to try to wait until morning when the nurses came on duty! I suffered through the rest of the night alone, and at 8:00 A.M., they called a cab to take me to the hospital.

In the labor room, I was left alone in terrible pain. Strange doctors and nurses came in periodically to check my progress, but nobody spoke. They just did their jobs. Finally a woman came in to sit with me. She seemed like an angel, but I suspect she was a volunteer. Holding my hand, she stayed for the rest of my labor, telling me that "everything will be fine" and "it won't last much longer."

I tried to be brave and never moaned or complained. That woman really made a difference for me. I wish I knew who she was. I would like to thank her.

I don't remember anything about the actual birth because they put me to sleep. When I awoke in the recovery room, the same woman was there. She took my hand and said I had had a baby boy.

"He's fine, dear. He was a little blue, but they gave him oxygen. Everything's okay now."

But it certainly wasn't. After I was taken to my hospital room, I developed a kidney infection and very high fever. I remember that everything seemed rather dream-like. A nurse stuck an I.V. in my arm and started me on antibiotics. A social worker from the home came by with some papers for me to sign. She said something about temporary custody, but I was too sick to even think. She said this needed to be done right away, so I signed.

After twenty-four hours on the antibiotics, I was feeling much better and called for a nurse. I asked to see my baby, but she just hemmed and hawed and would not give me a straight answer. I started crying and getting hysterical, demanding that they bring me my baby. Someone finally did but warned me that I was not allowed to feed him.

I'll never forget those few minutes I spent with my sweet baby. I opened the blanket and examined his perfect, beautiful little body. I counted all his fingers and toes. I told him that I loved him and that I was so sorry that I could not keep him. "I want to do what's best for you, darling. And I have no way of providing for you."

8

Bonnie

I gave him a name, Jon Steven. Then the nurse came and took him away. It was such a feeling of loss! I cried until I thought my heart would burst.

I was taken back to the home to recover. Five days after delivery, they took me to a judge's office to sign the surrender papers. The judge briefly explained the adoption laws and added that I had ninety days in which to change my mind. That was the very first time anyone had suggested that there might be other options.

A little flame of hope lit up inside me. Could I possibly keep my baby? But then I started thinking of the bleakness of my situation. I was eighteen years old with no husband and no job. I didn't want to disgrace my family. I wanted to do what I could to salvage their reputations. I didn't want my baby growing up as an inferior person, and besides, I wanted a husband and family some day. No decent man would have me if I had an illegitimate baby.

The social worker put her hand on my shoulder and said, "You're doing the right thing. Sign the papers."

I did. The next day I was driven to the bus station and was left there. Nobody even stayed with me to make sure I got on the right bus. I felt like they had gotten what they wanted, and now they were finished with me.

Daddy picked me up at our town's bus station. He gave me a kiss and drove me home. Nothing was said about my ordeal or the baby. The rest of my family welcomed me home, never guessing the real truth. For everyone except me, life went on as usual. Neither Mother nor Daddy ever mentioned my baby again.

Looking back on it now, I think my parents didn't talk about the baby because they thought it was best for me to forget about it and get on with my life. I had no idea how they really felt, but from then on Daddy always had a very sad look in his eyes. It's hard to describe, but nothing was ever the same between Daddy and me again. It wasn't anger but more of a deep hurt and disappointment in me, I think.

I used all my energy to try not to think about the baby. I did not discuss it with anyone. I never shared my pain with my friends, my family, or anyone. I tried to pretend that there wasn't any baby. But sometimes at night, alone in my room, my feelings would surface, and I would cry into my pillow.

I had always been fairly self-confident and assertive, but I wasn't the same person after that. I felt like whatever it was that made me Bonnie was gone. No matter what I accomplished or achieved, I never felt like it was good enough. I wasn't good enough. I always felt dirty, used and useless. Everything I did was just fake. I attended college for a while but dropped out for lack of interest more than anything. I worked halfheartedly at a mindless job.

The following spring, B.J. came back again, wondering if we could possibly work things out. We got married that summer, when my baby was ten months old. I never talked to B.J. about my deep feelings of grief about my baby, but I think he could tell that I was sad. By then, I actually had grown quite bitter. If my baby had been his, I wouldn't have had to surrender him! B.J. felt sorry for me, I think. He thought that another baby would help, so we started trying. We had been married barely a year when B.J. was killed in a car accident.

My mother died two months later. My terrible life just kept getting worse and worse! I was filled with resentment. If B.J. had been my baby's father, I would be a single mother and everybody in the world would rally around me, giving me all kinds of support to raise my child. That's the difference between "orphan" and "bastard" I guess. I still have a lot of anger about how things were back then. Nowadays, nobody understands what it was like for me.

I was a complete wreck. I didn't think things would ever get better. One of my aunts had a dear friend whose son had been injured in Vietnam. She came to visit me and commenced to say that it might be a good thing for me to befriend him, since we were both young people who had undergone great tragedies. Among his other injuries, Sam had lost a leg and part of one lung. I started visiting Sam in the hospital, and that's how I met my husband of twenty-four years.

We married and had a baby almost right away. Sheila was born the day after our first wedding anniversary. She was so beautiful! I cried because she looked exactly like my first baby. I cried because my mother hadn't lived long enough to see the baby I was going to be allowed to keep. I cried for all the sadness in my world.

In the midst of my sadness, Sheila was a complete joy. I barely let anyone else touch her. Determined to be a perfect mother, I seldom left her with a baby

Bonnie with her daughter and husband

sitter. When she was barely toddling, Sheila started fantasizing about having a big brother. She used to beg me for a big brother, and it would just tear my heart out.

Another reason for my sadness was my marriage. Things are much better now, but for many years our relationship was quite rocky. I won't go into specifics, but it had to do with Sam's war injuries and subsequent emotional problems. Anyway, I allowed things to happen that I shouldn't have. Given my lack of self-esteem at that time, I figured I didn't deserve any better.

But we continued as a family. Sam wanted to have another child. I did not want any more children. This is strange, but I was afraid that, if I had another child, it would be a boy. I did not want a boy. I think I was afraid that all the pain would come back if I had a boy.

I sold real estate for a couple of years, then went back to college and got a degree in accounting. When Sheila was nine, Sam finally badgered me into having another child. Well, I had a little boy and named him Wayne. And yes, all those memories came flooding back to me as I had feared. I held Wayne for almost the entire first three months of his life. I slept in a chair holding him. I thought about my first baby boy all the time, and it started making me a little crazy. I even went to a psychic to try to find out about where he was.

For the next few years, I thought and worried about my first baby constantly. I thought about the possibility of searching for him but didn't think I could cope with his rejection of me. So I decided I would never search for him, but I would welcome him with open arms if he ever wanted to find me. I wrote a letter to him in care of the Tennessee Human Services. I told him a little about our family and some medical information. The letter would be placed in his file. I felt more peaceful after making this final decision about him.

The years went by, and I pursued my career as an auditor. My job, raising the children, and coping with Sam's medical needs kept me quite busy. Five years before, Sam had to be put on kidney dialysis, which was an added strain.

One evening in 1996 at dinnertime, the phone rang. The voice on the other end said, "Is this Bonnie Keith?"

"Yes." For some reason, my heart began pounding.

"I'm from the Tennessee Department of Human Services, and I want to inform you about a change in the Tennessee adoption law."

I was speechless but finally pulled myself together enough to ask her to wait while I went to a more private phone. When I picked up again, I asked if this call had something to do with the son I had placed for adoption.

"Yes," she replied, "and would you be receptive to contact with him?"

"Yes." I told her that my daughter knew of her half brother but Wayne didn't. I was afraid of my first son calling and Wayne answering the phone. I asked if there would be an intermediary and would she tell me something about him. What was his name?

She refused to tell me anything. She said I needed to write a letter giving permission to release my identity. She suggested I rent a post office box if I didn't want him knowing my address at first.

I didn't sleep at all that night. I decided I wasn't going to rent a post office box. After all, this boy was my son. I wouldn't try to hide from him. I sent the letter of release the next day, Express Mail. In my letter, I asked if he could call me on Friday night. I would get the family to leave so we could talk in privacy.

The next few days were very difficult. I kept thinking, "What if he doesn't call? What if he's changed his mind?" I almost drove myself crazy with those kinds of thoughts.

Friday night finally came. I sent Sam and Wayne out to the movies. Sheila was away at college in Alabama. I waited by the telephone. At 8:30, the phone rang. And the most beautiful voice I had ever heard was on the other end. He sounded so much like my brother, I could not believe it! His name was Frank Jeffers, and he had lived in Tennessee his whole life. He had been trying to find me since he was eighteen. A former marine, he had served in the Gulf War. He was married and had a master's degree in accounting. What a coincidence. My degree was in accounting, too!

I could tell that he was well educated, polite and sweet. I loved him immediately. We talked for about two hours. Neither of us could believe how at ease we were with each other. We had so much in common!

I prepared a family photo album for Frank, with pictures of the kids and myself and some of when I was a child. I tried to include as many family members as possible. I mailed that to him the following Monday. In turn, he sent me current pictures of himself and his wife, Terri, and some pictures of his babyhood and childhood. I was amazed at how much he looked like me. His childhood pictures looked like a male version of me at the same ages!

My daughter and I were in close touch because we were planning her wedding at that time. When I told Sheila about being in contact with my first son, she was thrilled. The first thing she said was, "Well, is he a Christian? Can he come to my wedding?"

I had still not told Wayne about his half brother. Sam was very concerned that Wayne would somehow get hurt in all of this and asked me not to tell him. I agreed to put off telling him for awhile—just until I could find out if Frank really wanted to have a relationship with us, or if it was just curiosity. I did not want to put Wayne through any hurt. He was only twelve at the time.

Frank and I talked on the phone frequently for the next couple of weeks. Then we set up a meeting at a South Carolina hotel, located roughly halfway between our home in Georgia and his in Tennessee. Frank and Terri were already there when Sam and I arrived. We went to his room, but I didn't even get a chance to knock. He saw me through the window and came out to greet me with a dozen yellow roses.

We hugged each other tightly. This was undoubtedly the happiest moment of my life. The very happiest.

Sam and Terri were sweet and understanding. They disappeared for the evening, leaving Frank and me alone to talk. I held his hand almost the entire

Bonnie

time. I think I made him a little uncomfortable because I was staring at him so much, but I wanted to memorize every detail of his features. I was afraid that I would never see him again.

The next morning, the four of us went out to breakfast. I think Frank and I both knew by that time that we wanted to have a relationship. This was just too special for a single meeting.

Home again, I went over to Daddy's. "I've got something I need to tell you regarding my past—a young man. You probably know what I'm about to say."

He knew. "I thought this might happen," Daddy responded.

And then he went on to tell me how the loss of his grandson had affected him. Daddy said, "Not a single day has gone by that I don't think about that baby. I have prayed for him every night."

From then on, Daddy totally accepted Frank as part of the family.

When I told Wayne about his half brother, he thought it was a joke. He could not believe that his "straight" mother could have something like this in her past. When he realized I was serious, he was shocked but not angry. Now he and Frank are great buddies. They both love guitars and computers, and Frank is a wonderful role model for him. Sheila and Frank get along fairly well, although I think Sheila would like us all to be able to see him more often.

Sam has been extremely supportive through all this, and shares my happiness about being reunited with my first son.

Frank and I enjoy each other so much. It's like we know each other's hearts. We're so much alike, with similar views and similar ways of reacting. We tell each other everything—even the most private details of our lives. He says, "You understand me the way nobody else does."

14

Bonnie

I feel the same about him. We talk on the phone about once a week and visit via E-mail more often than that. The only problem is with his family. I've been trying to make friends with his adoptive mom and dad, but they seem reluctant. I've written letters thanking them for all they've done and asking to meet them, but have received a lukewarm response.

Frank doesn't want his grandparents to know about me because he's convinced they would never understand. I don't understand how I could be a threat to anybody. His adoptive mother had him exclusively for twenty-five years, and I could never compete with that. I wouldn't want to try. I figure, the more people a person can love and be loved by, the better.

Frank and Terri have a little boy now. My grandbaby! His name is Sheldon, and he's the sweetest little thing. My dearest wish is that I can be allowed to be a real grandma to him.

But as it stands right now, I'm kind of a "closet birth mom." I would like things to be different, and maybe everything will work out with time. It bothers me that I still feel so hurt and angry about what happened in my life. I'm hoping that I can eventually put all the anger and bitterness behind me. Somehow, though, I don't think that will ever happen.

* * *

Chapter Two

Laurel

Dance with Dad

Nothing fancy, it was like walking to him.
The Polka, the Schottische, my Mary Janes
scuffing his wing tips, his face
my Christmas tree top.

I knew all the steps. The accordion lady
played the Blue Skirt Waltz,
his hand and arm
the circle that turned us.

Full and humming, I knew the change would come.
On the day my father could no longer
touch me, I saw myself grown large and him
too solid for sentiment.

So the sky blows off its clouds.
After we grow up, we grow out.
After we grow out, we grow in.
It's always the loneliness that turns us.

I was a dreamy little kid, always pretending and fantasizing. I was "in a world of her own," according to the aunts who gave me manicure kits for Christmas so I would stop biting my nails. My dolls were my real family and the only ones who understood me. I had few human friends, preferring the company of neighborhood dogs and cats. I started writing poetry as soon as I could write. My first was, God made the birds, God made the bees / God made my mother and God made me. / God made my father, whom I love very much. / God made my brothers, and even my old tooth brush!

I've always had a great need to be understood. I wrote little books, illustrated them and bound them with pieces of ribbon or string. There were no other artists in our family, and I was referred to as the "different" one.

My mother, like her mother and sisters, had always been sentimental and caring. I remember how sorry she felt for me when I wasn't invited to a classmate's birthday party or was otherwise snubbed. My father was the strong, silent, hard-working type. Other than once a year at his labor union's Christmas dance, he spent most of his time at work in the foundry or at work in our garden. My mother helped with the weeding and canned all the vegetables and fruit they grew. Nothing went to waste.

I had two brothers. My older brother was the smartest, and my younger brother was the cutest. We all went to St. Joseph's Catholic School. I loved the mystery and drama of the priests and wanted to be one when I grew up. But I was just a girl, and girls had to be nuns, which didn't interest me much. Nuns didn't get to do the important things, like changing wine and wafers into the actual, "for-real" Body and Blood of Christ.

Other times, I felt second best when my friend Karen got a real Tiny Tears doll, and I got the cheaper imitation from Montgomery Wards. I desperately wanted the pearl-covered prayer book for First Communion, as well as the glimmering crystal rosary, but I had to settle for the less expensive models.

In ninth grade I was sure I was the only girl who wasn't allowed to shave her legs. I tried to wear knee-highs every day because I knew that people noticed. I dreaded gym class, when all the girls took off their clothes. The towels they gave us were way too small, and I knew my body was ugly. I tried to hold one towel in front and one in back when I went from my locker to the showers.

Everyone else seemed poised and relaxed about these things. Some even sang the song, "I'm in the nude for love . . . simply because you're near me . . . funny but—funny butt? Who's got a funny butt?"

I did pretty well in junior high and had a few friends—mostly quiet, uninspired girls. I did not have enough confidence to do well with boys. I did have one "boyfriend" of sorts. His name was Jim, and whenever I talked to him his ears turned red. He walked me home from school, but that was about it.

When I was a junior in high school, I fell in love with Mike, whom I met at the Safari Club, a teenage dance hall. Mike was a member of a very exotic and harmless gang, the Ptarmigans. Gangs in those days mostly hung out together, worked on their cars and lusted secretly after girls. Mike was a senior at another high school and picked me up at my school in his 1964 midnight blue Pontiac Grand Prix. I loved being seen with him and riding around in that beautiful car. I remember all sorts of feelings stirring around inside me, and I was not sure exactly what they were.

Mike was my first real boyfriend, and I knew we would be together forever. But after only a few months, he fell in love with my friend Lynne. At our parting date, he told me he was going to sell his car. His car! I couldn't believe it. And then, giving me a meaningful look, he said, "Everybody gets tired of everything after a while."

That time my mother really felt sorry for me. I cried constantly, refused to go to school and spent most of my time gazing out of windows. It felt good in a way, being involved in such a drama and having someone worry about me.

I wrote a poem about being made out of eggshell. There seemed to be something broken inside of me. I didn't care anymore. Not about what I was going to do after graduation, not about anything. It was as if I didn't matter anymore. I tried to make a plan. Even enrolled in college. But my heart was not in it. I do not know where my heart was.

In the blur of graduation events, I went through the motions, had my senior picture taken and had some fun with classmates. That summer I worked at a candy store and arranged my transportation to college. I had to commute from St. Paul to the small Wisconsin university because we could not afford the dorm. I thought I would major in English. Maybe teach some day.

I wrote poems about rolling down a hill of cotton. I did not feel alive. As if from a distance, I liked school and was doing fairly well but felt unfocused and lost. Slowly and deliberately, I discovered that sex felt good. I had a huge need to be touched and cared for. I thought that having sex meant somebody loved me. It did not take me long to find out how wrong I was.

Laurel

At college, after a day of drinking beer and playing cards when we were supposed to be in class, some boys I barely knew took me out to a dark parking lot and put me in the back seat of a car. Then they raped me, one after another. I think they drugged me because I was drifting in and out of consciousness. After what seemed like hours, one of the boys took pity on me, helped me locate most of my clothes and drove me home. I'm pretty sure that was when I got pregnant. It was October 22, 1965.

"What are you, some kind of whore?" was how my father responded to the news of my pregnancy.

My mother just cried, and then took me to a doctor because she wanted him to do something—I didn't know what. The doctor told my mother that it looked like I had been "treated roughly."

The Day I Died

I wanted to be beautiful, to be known for reading
between the possibilities,
when my borders were irrevocably crossed.

This was the wildness each spiral
feels as it twirls toward the edge.

The dome light clicked on when the door was
opened, off when the door was closed.
That strobe light effect made my arms look shorter
and someone else's naked legs.

The serious students took turns.
Sex was a subject they would never miss.
When I asked them to stop, they wouldn't.

Light on, light off. Tires trembled.
The dangling car freshener rocked.

I wanted them to know me beautiful
so I braced myself against the arm rest
and accepted one after another.
I was a length of pipe with the world passing through.

Parts of my body were cartooned
on desktops that semester.

19

Behind the newspaper, my father's face.
My mother made sure that no one
went hungry.

Bearer of corn and potatoes,
she beat the rugs regularly
and rolled each of her children
tight as a pair of socks.

Her slacks were woven with strands of agony.
Winged creatures served her berries.

No one is beautiful except mothers.
All little children raise their arms to be held.

Only violets and rhubarb are normal.
A flash of teeth, sickening roses,
they remind me of the day I died.

I quit college, and never told my parents what really happened. I just
let them believe whatever they wished. My whole life was a lie anyway. Mom
made up stories about my visiting a cousin in Ohio. In reality, they signed me
up with a Catholic social service agency. Then came some unsuccessful
attempts at being a "girl" in various households. As such, I was supposed to
work for my keep, with chores that ranged from babysitting for ten children to
scrubbing a bathroom with bleach every day. I hated doing other people's work
and was eventually placed in a home for unwed mothers.

Boys called the place "Watermelon Hill" and drove by in their cars
yelling rude comments. I was not allowed contact with anyone except my parents. On weekends when my folks brought me home for a visit, I had to lie on
the floor of the car, belly and all, so none of the neighbors would see me. All
the shades in the house were drawn.

The "home" was everything I expected, complete with bars on the
windows and dormitory cots. The nuns who ran the place spent mornings in
chapel praying for our redemption. At the home, they gave us each a fake
name made up of our real initials. My fake name was Laurel Taylor. We were
not supposed to tell each other our real names. Mother Superior whisked up

and down the halls, her black cloak flapping. We called her "the old bat," but everyone was afraid. She had the power to double—or triple—our chores, which included tasks like scrubbing the many steep wooden stairways, waxing the auditorium floors, and scraping garbage off one hundred plates.

Laurel

They kept us busy because obviously the devil had taken hold of us at least once and, heaven knows, he might get us again. When I could get away with it, I stayed in bed as much as possible, reading e.e. cummings, listening to Bob Dylan and writing page after page of poetry.

Babies were being born right and left. The girl in the cot on my left had twins. She kept them. Most girls were going to place their babies for adoption. I wasn't sure about what to do.

I loved my baby even before I felt him move inside me. Having this baby was a good and important thing. In fact, it was the first important thing I had ever done. The chapel was a good place to get away from everybody, and I ended up praying for guidance. When I realized that my baby was more important than my life, it became clear that I needed to give him up for adoption. Everything about me was a wreck. I couldn't offer him a decent future.

Time never moved so slowly. My favorite song was Paul Simon's "I Am a Rock." I wondered how to protect myself like that.

Finally, on a sunny day in July, the pains began. A taxi took me to the hospital. I can't remember if my mother was there or not. I think not, because I didn't want her there. There were women moaning and screaming in nearby rooms. I remember thinking how melodramatic they were. I never screamed or called out.

Shadow Mothers

I had a baby boy and named him Jeffrey Phillip Taylor. I thought it was a manly and sensitive name. He came a little early and was slightly jaundiced, but otherwise he was fine, they told me. I wanted to see him. The nurses refused. After a few days, we were both brought separately back to the home, and I made a fuss until they let me see him. I think I could have killed someone if they would have kept refusing my request. I'm not ordinarily fierce, but I was then.

I was put in a small white room with a white wooden rocking chair, and my baby was brought to me. He looked like a little angel, all sweet and soft. In the eerie white glow, I held him, rocked him, took off all his clothes and checked to make sure he was perfect. My mother had seen him through the glass at the hospital nursery. Looking at him had changed her mind entirely, and she wanted me to keep him. But I said no and kissed him good-bye. Honestly, I don't know how I was so strong.

I made up a beautiful story about the baby's father for the social worker. I said he was Swedish, in case the baby turned out to be blonde. (I had dark hair.) I claimed the father was a straight-A student because I wanted to make sure the baby would go to college. I made it sound like the father and I had a long term, though ill-fated, relationship.

I don't even remember signing the papers, but I must have. The social worker told me to go home and start my life all over again. I went home, told more lies and got an office job. I moved away from home as soon as I could. Being with my family in that house was no good. I wanted to move on—to grow up or something.

I liked sharing an apartment with other girls, but they seemed so well adjusted, so "together." And I had this huge, ragged hole inside me. I cried for my baby every night—and for many years afterwards.

Making money became my top priority. I had to make enough to get out of town. I had to move on. California sounded good. My older brother was in the navy, stationed in the San Francisco area. I wouldn't be totally alone.

To get enough money for an airplane ticket, I worked at a bank during the day and as a go-go dancer at night. As was the style in that era, I danced in a little cage. I wore a black leotard, net stockings, sleeveless sweater and a blonde wig. At the bank my uniform was a green suit. It all fit perfectly with my double life, pretending to be myself but feeling like someone else inside.

Laurel

With 500 dollars in traveler's checks, I moved to San Francisco and got a room in a slightly run-down hotel. Every few days, I had my room changed to a less expensive one. I ate peanut butter sandwiches and apples and cried myself to sleep every night. Because of his duties, my brother rarely had time to see me. San Francisco wasn't any better than home. It was only lonelier.

After Saying Good-bye to My Baby I

When I was free in San Francisco
my plan of action was written in the sand
with one thin finger while the wind already
gathered to rework my fate.
The money saved from working two jobs
saved me from working for three months.
Too shy to talk, I took the bus to Sunset
where the unemployed fed pigeons
and wove gods-eyes and each day gave up
its ghostly hue by sliding into the sea.
Then back to my closet room with the bath
down the hall and the TV room where
I sat with the old and lost watching Dragnet reruns.
I was that girl I never knew and nobody wanted,
afraid of the hills, that they might tip over,
the pain of missing my baby pouring from my eyes.
At night in my bed I would hold him, my pillow.
I did not know how my life could go on
but I knew his would. Did he miss me?
Would he think me silly to kiss this?

My brother introduced me to his neighbor, Brad, who was even more lost than I was. Brad's mother was manic-depressive, and years later he was diagnosed as chronically depressed. We became hippies together, dropped acid on the weekends and attended anti-war demonstrations in Berkeley. We spent long evenings at my place making love and listening to The Doors, Cream, and Big Brother & The Holding Company. Oddly conservative hippies, we both held full time jobs during the week.

Brad and I decided to get married almost immediately. Actually, I think it was me who decided. We hadn't even known each other six weeks. My mother was thrilled and, I think, relieved that I had finally found someone. I flew home, planned a quick wedding and went through with it, even though I had my doubts. We were married on March 16, 1968, the day of the My Lai massacre during the war in Vietnam. I flew back to Mountain View, California, with my new husband. I wore a big diamond and had hopes to match.

Things were never very good between us, although we did love each other after a fashion. We both had too many needs. My biggest need was to have a baby—one I could keep. We moved back to Minnesota because it was a better place to raise children. I got a job as a bank teller and soon was ecstatic to find myself pregnant. I couldn't wait to wear maternity clothes and start crocheting little booties and bonnets.

As was our summer custom, my mother and I went to visit my great aunt Louise who lived on the family farm in Wisconsin. Aunt Paula was there, too. "Life is so good," gushed Aunt Paula. "My life has been so much fun . . . don't you wish you could just go back and do it all again?"

Aunt Louise leaned back in the rocker and answered, "I'd never want to live through all of that again."

I was shocked. I thought she had been happy. I made some comment about being happy now that I was finally going to have a baby. And Aunt Louise looked at me closely and said, "You shouldn't count on anything."

Maybe Aunt Louise was psychic or maybe it was fate, but I lost that baby at five months. The nurses said it was a blessing because something was wrong with it. But for me, it was an unbearable curse. Sorting through all the soft little garments, my heart was worse than broken—it had died with the baby. Brad didn't know what to do with me, so he got me some anti-depressant medication. I remember not being able to get the child-proof cap open and spilling the pills all over the tile floor, where they scattered like a shotgun blast. Then I sat on the bathroom floor watching the faucet, drop after drop.

Later that year, Monica was conceived. Everything went well, and I finally had my baby. She was my absolute joy. I poured my soul into her. Things were still not very good between Brad and me, but we both tried very

24

hard. For the next several years we attended counseling. I started reading self-help books in addition to Dr. Spock.

Jed was born when Monica was three. The children were my life. They were enchanting, intelligent, gorgeous, wonderful. I became active in a parent-cooperative preschool program, church, and neighborhood activities. But I still had that empty hole inside me caused by the loss of my first son. I knew then that other children couldn't fill his space. I wrote to the adoption agency periodically, and they sent me "non-identifying" information about him. It didn't really help, so I tried harder to forget about him.

Having replaced ourselves in the world, Brad and I decided not to give birth to any more children. But I wanted one more child. I began exploring international adoption, and Carrie came into our family from Korea six months after we made application. She arrived on July 16, 1975, three days after Monica's fifth birthday, and the exact day of my first son's ninth birthday. I could never have planned for that to happen! I wondered if God was giving me some sort of sign.

Things seemed better, except for the increased stress of having two children in diapers and a weak marriage. I think that I changed, and Brad stayed the same. At some point, maybe because of my social activities, new feminist friends, or through some internal maturation process, I made a conscious decision to be happy. I decided not to be some wimpy woman at the mercy of whatever the fates dished out any longer. I was going to make a life for myself, no matter what. I knew if things stayed the way they were, I would die. I would just shrivel up and die. We broke up and got back together several times. Finally, I asked him to move out permanently.

The kids—especially Monica—hated me after the divorce. She was old enough to believe that the divorce was her fault. I worked very hard to reassure them all, but Jed stuttered for a long time, and Carrie wouldn't sleep through the night. Sometimes the tensions built up inside me, and I was afraid I might hurt the kids. So I would lock myself in the bathroom until I felt stronger.

It was hard, being a single parent all those years. I knew it wasn't the worst thing that had ever happened to me, but it was right up there. But believe it or not, there was a bright side. When I made a decision, there was no one to argue with me.

Brad was always dependable with the child-support payments, bless his heart. I located some part-time work at first, and then a series of jobs to make ends meet.

I wanted my kids to have as much love and nurturing as possible, and I didn't care who gave it to them. There was no way I could handle all their needs alone. Brad's emotional problems made it difficult for him to give affection. I found Carrie a mentor family who had two adopted Korean kids. We are forever grateful for their love and companionship—and for Jed's "big brother" too, who boosted his self-confidence and encouraged him in outdoor activities.

After some research, I found a program that guided me through vocational testing, and I talked my way into the advertising industry, where I eventually got a job as a writer. How wonderful! Whoever thought that I could make a living doing what I loved best? What a kick that was—going to work every day thinking, "Wow. I am a real writer!"

Ironically, now I was popular with men. Some, though, wouldn't date me because I had children. As the old story goes, I kissed quite a lot of frogs before I found my prince. But find him I did. My best friend, my confidant, my strongest supporter, my soul mate, Dave.

Primer
Three years are long enough to learn
how to count, brush up and down,
get toilet trained.
Long enough to start thinking
Mister Rogers is dumb.
Three years are long enough
to outgrow Cinderella bedrooms,
animal slippers and nite lites.
For a smashed fingernail to grow back,
magic marker to wear off.
Long enough to lather peanut butter
between thick slices of loss—
a single parent, lonely enough
to learn from children the secrets

of horsies in marshmallow clouds,
the creamy center of a Twinkie.
Long enough to turn around and find
the man who finds horsies, windmills,
angels and unicorns
making peanut butter sandwiches
in your kitchen with your children
like he wants to marry you.

Dave and I gave the kids plenty of time to get used to the idea of our marriage. Monica was eleven, just the right age to question my every action. I thank my mother for taking her aside and telling her, "Your mother deserves to be happy. You want your mother to have someone who loves her, don't you?" Eventually, each of the children worked out their own individual arrangements for getting along with and learning to love Dave. Beth, his daughter from a previous marriage, didn't live with us but was an important part of the picture, too. There were a lot of relationships to handle!

With Dave and me, the honeymoon lasted a long time. Even now, more than eleven years later, we're still nuts about each other. My newfound happiness was a boost to my creative capabilities—and I began to publish my poems in many literary journals and magazines, while at the same time progressing in my advertising writing career.

The children grew from stage to stage, presenting an array of challenges along the way. All three were teenagers at the same time! Dave's daughter Beth was a brilliant student who eventually graduated from a private New York City college and got a job as an editor in the publishing industry. Monica, also a brilliant student, achieved a graduate degree, travels extensively and is a teacher. Jed stumbled a bit in high school but then graduated with a high grade point average from a technical school and found a perfect niche for himself in computer-aided design. Carrie is still in college where she is blossoming, volunteering for Habitat for Humanity, making new friends and figuring out what her future holds.

Life was busy, and the pain of losing my first son faded into the background. The last update I requested and received was when he was fifteen.

They said he was tall and handsome, a high school football star and avid hunter and fisherman. They said he liked to write stories. My feelings of loss never really healed but sort of scabbed over.

One day in 1986, an art director with whom I worked told me about how she had recently found her birth son, due to the fairly recent changes in Minnesota adoption laws. It suddenly occurred to me, "Hey, I bet I could find my son."

As mentioned earlier, I had kept in touch with the adoption agency over the years, but it was never suggested that I could ever actually meet him.

When I decided to try, it all became unbelievably easy. After the obligatory face-to-face meeting with a social worker, the agency called the phone number they had on file. His family had moved but just down the block. He had lived in the same small Minnesota town his whole life.

His immediate response to their query was, "Sure! I've always wanted to meet her!"

We were at Carrie's soccer banquet the night Tim, my son, was due to call me for the first time. I could barely eat and excused myself early to wait for the phone to ring. I sat at the edge of the bed. His voice was unfamiliar, strange. He was a real person, a grown man. I did not think either of us could wait. We decided to meet the following Thursday, at a restaurant halfway between his college and the ad agency where I worked.

The days dragged by. I was obsessed with the idea of being able to see my son after all the years. I could think of nothing else. All the years of pain, all the feelings roared around in my head. My dear family was very patient with me.

He looked beautiful and strangely familiar. He hugged me stiffly, and I could tell that, like my dad, Tim did not wear his heart on his sleeve. Sitting across the table from each other, neither of us could stop staring. The words poured out of both of us. He told me he was grateful to me for giving him such a good life. I was relieved that he hadn't felt unwanted or abandoned by me. I told him how I had held him and kissed him good-bye. He took my hand. He cried. We both cried. He showed me a picture of himself at seventeen as best man in his brother's wedding. I felt the deep loss of all the years I had missed.

Laurel

Shadow Mother and Son Reunion

At 5:00 P.M. on November 13, they drove cars from separate cities.
He couldn't have looked more fragile,
at Eduardo's, twenty years old in his red letter jacket.
On shaky Levi legs he stood to greet her for the first time.
Shadow mother and son meet at last.

Together they ate a whole meal of their lives on white plates,
full circles. Nothing he told her was new.
Everything she said was true as the slash of sun
that resolves the night.

Her finger traced his nail's familiar shape—
two hands that, but for endless leaps of time,
should have known each other like gloves.
Together they broke crusts off bread,
watched the butter melt.

And what he didn't know was, this time
leaving him again, she wept miles in the car,
for what is new in the sky's full promise—
what is alive beyond belief.

After Tim and I met, there was a flurry of letters and phone calls and visits. The two of us took long walks around the lake. He is a middle child of three, just like me. His parents have similar personalities to my parents.

He told me that he had often thought and guessed things about me. Tim was always so caring and respectful of my feelings. He never even asked about his birth father, but I knew he must have been wondering. I finally worked up the courage to tell him about the rape.

Then I quickly added, "But I always thought of you as good—there was never anything bad about you."

His only response was to put his arm around my shoulders. We never talked about it again.

Tim was extremely interested in meeting his half siblings, especially Carrie, with whom I think he felt a special connection, since she was adopted as well.

When I told my kids about him, it was difficult for them at first. I think they feared they'd lose their places in the family. But it all smoothed over with time.

Laurel and family

His parents were concerned too, and I wrote them many letters to assure them that I was not going to insinuate myself into their family—that I respected them and thanked them for their good job in raising him. I was just so happy to know him. That big empty spot inside was finally filled.

The day Dave and I met his parents, we pulled into their driveway on our big black motorcycle wearing leather jackets. I figured, "This is me. I might as well not play any games. Either they'll like me or they won't."

His parents were very polite and served us cool drinks on the couch. His mother had his baby book and photo album on the coffee table for me. How thoughtful! She also gave me whatever photos I wanted from the album. There was a picture of him as a baby with his older brother. Pictures of him in grade school. I kept saying, "Oh, can I have this one? This one?"

"Of course," she replied.

I treasure those photos and wonder if I would have been as generous.

Laurel

When I told my mom and dad that I had found Tim, they were very happy for me. They knew how much pain I had endured over the years. Dad and I have never really discussed any of what happened. Mom tends to be a lot more open about emotions, and we're starting to talk about it. Better late than never, I guess. Maybe it's because of time and maturity, but I'm closer to my parents now than I've ever been.

For a time, all I could think about was Tim. I must have filled hundreds of journal pages with all my feelings. It was like a love affair of sorts. I could not get enough of him. I couldn't stop staring at him. He was my self, my core, mine, me. I compare it to how I felt in the hospital after Monica was born. She was me and I was her. Dave was very patient with this ongoing obsession of mine. I'm very grateful to him for that. Meeting my son was the biggest joy, like winning the lottery or having one's greatest wish come true.

Some part of me still misses everything I missed with Tim and still feels that he should have been with me. Intellectually, I know it was all for the best, but somehow my feelings don't quite match. There is a sort of bitterness or deep sadness. Writing this has taught me many things, and one is that I am still scarred by the whole experience. I thought I was over it, but I may never be.

Tim graduated from college with the intention of teaching social studies to junior high school kids and being an athletic coach. He married Angie, a girl from a nearby town. Mom and I were invited to Angie's bridal shower. Mom, Dad, Dave, and I attended the wedding. His family even gave me a corsage to wear! Mom and I both cried through the whole ceremony. She held my hand. At the reception, the photographer took a picture of Tim and me for their wedding album.

Tim is my only child who looks like me. He's the only one in his adopted family who likes to write stories. He's probably as stubborn as I am, too. The job market for teachers was tough. After a long search, summers spent laying sod, and winters of substitute teaching, he never gave up looking for a job in his field. Instead he shifted gears, got his special education certification and is now happily teaching at a suburban high school and coaching football.

Tim and Angie share dinners, ball games, and other events with the family and us. Tim has a slow, easy sense of humor and warm nature, like his adoptive father—and my father. He can be very funny, especially when he doesn't know it. We love Angie, who is a beautiful, sensitive and talented young woman. She is a perfect partner for him, and they're totally devoted to each other. She helps him remember my birthday and Mother's Day. She tells me that he loves and respects me and brags about me to his friends—things that he doesn't say to me. I think he loves me as a very special aunt. It's hard to put a name on the love connected with this relationship.

After Saying Good-bye to My Baby II

These hills are friendly to my legs now,
not tipping me over, nor calling my bluff.
I am not afraid of the cable car this time,
but grab a handful of my husband's shirt
as we career seemingly into the sea.
Too many times I have thought it safe
to walk my dog to visit every tree,
to examine too closely the past.
I have always known in which direction
the sea lies, as I know the difference
between dream and earthquake.
I know my son now and he is tall,
with my eyes and part of my pain.
It is safe to kiss him now but touch
is not much to fill up twenty years.
This is just another city of flowers
and hoopla designed for the old and lost.
I know my way around this time.

People tell me that I did a great job as a mother, but I sure can't take all the credit. My children's lives are as happy and worthwhile as any of us can wish, and our connections together are very strong. They believe in themselves and are kind people. Brad and I did some things right together, and one of them was that we never made the children choose between us. We agreed that they deserved to love both of us. We both put their welfare before our emotions and anger. We weren't perfect, but we always tried to work together for the benefit of the children.

Laurel

All my children have moved out of the house now. That makes me happy and sad at the same time. After all, I didn't raise them to stay with me their whole lives, and now I can put more time into my writing. Still, they've always been a huge part of who I am, and I miss them.

Dave and I have wonderful adventures together. We travel whenever possible—motorcycle trips to Wisconsin and trips to Europe, Mexico, and Jamaica. We flew to San Francisco to see Monica receive her master's degree. The Bay Area has changed almost as much as I have. I never believed my life would be this happy or full.

Tim and Angie have moved out of the city for now. He's in his glory at their little lake home—hunting, fishing and doing all the outdoor things he loves. So far, neither of them minds the commute. Angie is the volunteer coordinator at an English learning school for immigrants and refugees. I volunteer there, teaching a writing class—so she's my boss! She thinks that's pretty funny.

Once in a while, Tim drops in at school after my class. Angie has told me that he would like to be closer to me. Of course he'd never come right out and say that to me. But that's fine. I understand. His hugs have become a lot less stiff, and sometimes, he walks up to me and kind of brushes my shoulder —which reminds me of the little nudges Dad used to give Mom when he passed her in the kitchen. Love is love; it doesn't have to be shouted from the rooftops.

For years now, I've been dreaming about babies almost every night. They're not exactly recurring dreams, because each dream is different. I dream about brown babies, white babies, the powder smell of them, my babies, other women's babies, dressing babies, finding babies in the jungle, rescuing babies from rubble, babies floating on clouds and just holding them in my arms. A friend told me these dreams mean that I am helping babies move from one world into another. I don't know about that, but I do feel responsible. And I do love them so.

* * *

Chapter Three

~ *Arlene* ~

My dad was on a ship somewhere in the North Atlantic when I was born at the naval hospital in Norfolk, Virginia, in June 1943. Since he did not come home for good until World War II ended, for the first three years of my life I was raised by my mom and her parents, who immigrated to the United States from Vienna, Austria. They fled their country just before the war, and since Austria was an Axis country, they had been listed as enemy aliens. I can't picture that sweet group of people as enemy aliens!

We all lived in Washington, D.C., in my grandparents' home. The family was very European—very close. My mother was the center of my universe. I loved her so much. Maybe too much. I hung on her every word and believed in her completely. Although there was little extra money, we always made a big deal over birthdays, Christmas, and other holidays. Inexpensive or homemade presents were always being passed around.

Mom and my grandparents disciplined verbally and very gently. When I was bad, they would scold me or send me to my room, but they never hit; they didn't believe in physical punishment. They never even raised their voices.

When Dad came home and we moved to Arlington, Virginia, I was terrified of him, especially at first. He believed in spanking, slapping, yelling, and screaming when he was angry. Then it would be over, and he would be fine again. This was quite the contrast to my soft-spoken mother.

I hated my dad's explosive German-Irish temper. But he could also be very loving and affectionate. Dad was always ready with bunches of hugs and kisses for me, and then for my sister Polly, who was born when I was five, and Peter, who came along three years later.

34

Arlene

We grew up in a sleepy little neighborhood that was slightly southern, very conservative. In those days, northern Virginia around the Arlington area was mostly homes, shops, churches, schools. Our smallish home always seemed to be overflowing with kids and our friends. We rode bikes, played in the woods, built forts and pretended we were soldiers. It was a basic happy childhood. Until I started school, that is.

From the time I was very young, I remember people saying I had "two left feet" because I would trip over almost anything, walk into door frames and walls, and just be generally clumsy. It wasn't until I was in my forties that I was diagnosed as severely learning-disabled. It was found that I had many related problems, including double vision.

As one might imagine, grade school was horrible. I couldn't have possibly understood how I was different from everyone else. School was so much harder for me than it should have been. Unless I really strained, I saw two of everything, side by side. I couldn't sit still. My attention span and recall were nil. I constantly mixed up numbers and couldn't remember directions. If I wasn't physically shown how to do something, I couldn't follow even the simplest of instructions. Everything I was able to learn, I learned by listening and memorizing.

Whenever I was tested, the teachers would say, "The tests show that she's brilliant. She should be an "A" student, rather than just getting by. She must be lazy. She spends too much time daydreaming and too little time paying attention!"

Unfortunately I believed them, which didn't do much for my self-confidence. I was so discouraged! It seemed like the harder I tried, the farther I fell behind—while my friends went ahead of me by leaps and bounds.

I was lucky I had so many friends. Those friendships brought me a lot of happiness. My best friends were Connie, DeeDee, Molly, and Marcia. Connie and I were practically inseparable from kindergarten until she moved away when we were about twelve. DeeDee and Molly were best friends with each other, and Marcia came along for the ride. She ended up being the smartest of us all—taking all the advanced classes and eventually going to Spain as an exchange student. Of all those childhood friendships, Marcia and I are the only ones who have remained close.

Although I hated school because of all the frustrations, I did love music and singing. I found that I was good at acting, most Girl Scout activities, and athletics. And, even though it was hard, I loved learning!

I know now that I must have been a near genius to find all the ways I did to adapt—and actually learn. And it was fortunate that I grew up in an era where reading aloud to the class was a big part of every day. If I could hear it, I could "get" it.

My hopes and dreams for my life were not extravagant. I wanted to get married, raise a family and be a housewife just like my mom. I think I would have been happy doing just that, but things didn't work out quite that way.

I guess it's no surprise that I wanted to follow in Mom's footsteps. She was highly organized, softly opinionated and had a tremendous inner strength. I relied on her judgment and was in awe of her abilities. I admired everything about her. She was the very best cook, and I loved to be in the kitchen with her. Mom had tons of patience with my clumsy ways. She allowed me to help cook the meals, cakes, cookies, pies—everything. We were very close. Mom had a way of making life fun.

Our tradition on Christmas Eve was to share a European "cold supper." I loved helping get ready for this day. The house would be cleaned top to bottom. We set up the Christmas tree and put all the wrapped presents under it. Mom and I made the meal together. All the cold cuts and special Austrian dishes we'd prepared were placed on the table. I always made the chicken livers all by myself because Mom didn't like them.

"Ach!" she'd say. "Don't care for them!"

Mom was wonderful. At supper, in the midst of all our hilarity, she would tell everyone which dishes I had made, saying "Aren't they just the best this year?"

I am so grateful to Mom for giving me confidence in my kitchen abilities. I still feel like there's nothing I can't do in the kitchen!

After supper on Christmas Eve, we would take hours opening presents— one at a time, making a big production out of each one. Then it was time to clean up and off to midnight service at church. Christmas Day was spent at Dad's parents' home, with a formal turkey dinner and more presents. Then we all played Michigan Rummy for pennies.

Arlene

Something else that still brings a smile is our family's camping vacations. What a riot! There was my organized mom, with lists of what everyone was to bring. Each of us was responsible for getting our own things together and packing them into boxes, which we hauled out to the 1955 Chevy station wagon. Then there was my dad, having a cow trying to fit everything in, and the kids making fun of him behind his back without getting caught! Finally, after the car was packed, we were settled in with pillows, books, and games, and off we went.

The next scene was "Putting Up the Tent," starring Mr. Temper and Mrs. Cool. Eventually Dad's sense of humor would overtake his temper, and he'd smile at us and yell, "Charge!"

He would then plunge into the tent with the center pole, and the tent would be up in a flash. That was his signal to go off and fish for the next two weeks. His daily appearances would occur at breakfast, when he presented us with his first catch of the day, and then again at dinner. He always went to bed early, and the three of us stayed up playing cards with Mom.

Junior high school was worse than grade school. It was transition time— time to question everything. I'm sorry to admit it, but, for the first time, I doubted my mother's judgment. My mother—whom I loved and respected above all others!

As I mentioned, Mom was an immigrant who arrived in this country at thirteen and didn't understand this culture. She had no idea how important it was for a girl my age to dress like the other girls. She didn't understand it was crucial to "look right." Instead, she picked out the worst clothes—clunky shoes and garish-colored socks. Because I never had much confidence in my own opinions, I didn't know how to tell her that I hated those clothes, that they made me look like a square. I mean, couldn't she see that everybody was wearing saddle shoes and bobby socks?

High school was better. I tried out for choir and was accepted. My classes were still very puzzling for me, so most of the time I just got by. I had reached the point where I realized it didn't really matter if I studied or not. I listened as the class discussed each subject, and I remembered only so much. Then I would get confused. Surprisingly, I was able to maintain a "C" average.

Shadow Mothers

One of the great sadnesses of my life was when my mother's mother died. This was the grandma with whom I had lived as a baby, and I loved her very much. I was only sixteen and believed that I had caused her death. I had become very ill with mononucleosis and yellow jaundice, and was on complete bed rest. I was sure that I had somehow passed my illness on to her—or because I required so much attention, she didn't get the attention that would have saved her life.

The real story is that tuberculosis had left her with one-third lung function, among other problems. Because of good medical care, she lived for another twenty years. Then she had to have surgery when her bladder failed. The heart specialist feared that she might not survive the surgery, but she did. Six weeks later she died of heart failure. It was all kind of jumbled, but for a long time afterwards, I blamed myself for her death. I was grief-stricken, and never really got over the loss.

Most families in the 1940s and 1950s did not discuss sex. I knew how cats reproduced but was never taught about human reproduction or sexuality. At one family event after my sister and I were adults, Mom swore that she had told us everything. At that, Polly and I looked at each other and rolled our eyes, laughing. We had known nothing. And we were afraid to ask. Maybe it was because of my continuing fear of my father's anger, or maybe it was some unspoken taboo or religious thing.

We attended church every Sunday. Apart from family activities, our social events were mainly church-related. I enjoyed all the church things just fine until I discovered boys. When we were about fourteen, DeeDee, Molly, Marcia, and I had make-out parties in our basement, the lights low and the music sexy and slow. A wide variety of boys from school were always eager to attend. The excitement of the forbidden made it all the more enticing for us. Beer was easy to get; we always had a great time and never got caught. We usually went out as a group, breaking into couples to go parking or to drive-in movies. Although we really had no idea what we were doing, our social lives revolved around sex.

When we discussed it among ourselves, we agreed that if anyone ever asked us to actually have intercourse, we would say no. We knew that if you did "it" you'd get pregnant.

38

Arlene

That time of my life is difficult to explain. Although I did like myself as a person, I felt inferior to all the kids with whom I hung around, thinking they were so much smarter than I. I carried around the guilt of my grandmother's death and missed her terribly. Somehow, I decided that sex would help me feel better. I was sixteen. I convinced myself that I needed to do "it." I looked over my circle of boyfriends and picked out a likely candidate. The rest was easy, and I was lucky enough to not get pregnant.

During my senior year of high school, I took a night class at a local university. There was a young man in my class who was very attractive to me. His name was Anthony, and he was a

Arleen at sixteen

full-time student, majoring in sociology. Anthony assumed that I was a college student too, and I never told him I was still in high school. We went to his apartment two or three times a week and had great sex. Anthony would then take me home in his white Jaguar XKE. He was as cool as his car, and I was crazy about him.

On graduation night, Chuck, a boy I knew from my homeroom class, asked me to go out with him after graduation exercises. I jumped at the chance, having always thought of him as drop-dead gorgeous. We went parking in his car, drank way too much beer and ended up having sex.

The next morning was filled with activity, because our family was moving to a new house. It was a bigger, much nicer home, and I looked forward to all sorts of happy times in it.

I hadn't been paying any attention to the regularity of my periods. After all, I had been sexually active for a long time, and I hadn't gotten pregnant, so I wasn't worried. But by the end of July, I knew I was pregnant.

I called Anthony to tell him, and his answer was, "It couldn't be me. I've been sterile since a diving accident in Hawaii. Have you been with anyone else?"

I panicked and hung up. Now that I look back on it, I was foolish to have believed him. I still don't know if he told me the truth or not. People were always taking advantage of me like that.

The rest of the summer passed in a sick daze. I was having morning sickness and sometimes evening sickness, too. I hibernated in the "rec room" of our nice new house. I did nothing and told no one about my problem.

Since I wasn't showing yet, I even started college in the fall, living at home and pretending nothing was wrong. When Mom confronted me in October, my pregnancy was pretty hard to deny. I was about five months along, and starting to pop out. My parents were very upset. They both cried. Mom said that she wished I had told her sooner, so that she could try to arrange an abortion through her contacts in Europe. Abortion was still illegal here in this country.

"Or," Mom said, "I could have pretended to be pregnant myself, so we could keep the baby."

I'm not sure that I could have lived with either of those options. I believed Anthony about not being the father, and I certainly didn't want to marry Chuck, who had gotten me drunk and used me.

I was afraid to tell my parents that Chuck was the father, in case they tried to force me to marry him. They kept after me, though, and eventually I gave in and told them about Chuck and how it happened. My father called Chuck's father and told him that he'd take care of everything but that Chuck's father should know what his son had done.

Mom and Dad took me to our pastor's office. Everybody acted like I was invisible. My parents and the pastor made the decision that my baby would be adopted. The pastor suggested a specific adoption agency, and my parents knew people who had adopted through this agency. They knew of one particular agency that did a thorough investigation of prospective parents. They wanted my baby to be raised in our Lutheran religion by loving parents.

Arlene

The next thing I knew, I was being sent to a home for unwed mothers in a town near Arlington. When I first got there, I was in some kind of shock or complete denial. I barely looked pregnant, didn't feel pregnant, and certainly didn't want to be pregnant at eighteen! But there I was, with about twenty-five other girls who were all in the same boat.

At first I didn't bathe very often because my towels kept disappearing. As usual, people were taking advantage of me. Everything was pretty grim until Lynn arrived. She took me under her wing and taught me how to fend for myself. She also taught me how to do laundry and how to protect my towels. I guess it was obvious that I'd never been away from home. Then, when Karmen arrived, Lynn and I took charge of her. She was in worse shape emotionally than I had been. The three of us became very close. Lynn and I remained friends for years. She was one of the best friends I've ever had.

There were strict rules at the home. We had to sign in and out and were required to eat all our meals together. We weren't supposed to exchange names and addresses, but Lynn, Karmen, and I did. It was a strange way to live. We were all just waiting to give birth and then get on with our lives.

Lynn had a girl and decided to keep her baby. I felt so lonely after she left. One day a social worker came to visit. She did some psychological tests on me, but she didn't counsel me, give me alternatives to adoption or suggest I could keep my baby.

I was trying to be a good girl, to get back into everyone's good graces, and I felt like this was God's punishment for having sex—having to give my baby up. My pastor and my mother told me that adoption was the right thing to do. And I really didn't even know how to question my mother's judgment.

Interestingly, despite the trauma, I look back on that time as one of the happiest of my whole life. I loved the feeling of being pregnant. I really enjoyed it. The only way I can explain it is that I felt at peace with the world.

Back home, my predicament was a "Big Secret." My sister and brother had no idea what was going on, and none of my friends knew. My parents and Dad's parents came to visit occasionally, and Mom called me on the phone every day. My dear grandfather took me out to dinner every Sunday, but he never said much.

The doctors thought my due date was in February, but February came and went—no baby. Of course, who knew exactly when I had become pregnant? My labor pains finally started on the afternoon of March 3, 1962. I was sent to the hospital alone. I remember watching a doctor show on TV during the first part of my labor, which wasn't very painful at all, and thinking, "Hey, this isn't so bad!"

It was decided that I wasn't progressing quickly enough, so my labor was induced. I was taken to the delivery room and heavily sedated. I don't remember a thing, but I was told that my daughter was born at 12:10 A.M. on March 4.

When I woke up, I felt like I had been cut in half. It was so awful. But then the nurses started bringing my baby in for all the regular feedings, and I forgot all about the pain. What a quiet and beautiful baby she was! For the next few days I held her and fed her. It was wonderful. I even had my mother crochet a little outfit for her.

I lied to my roommate about my situation, pretending I was a happily married young woman whose husband was, unfortunately, out of town when I went into labor. I didn't want her to think I was a slut.

On the fourth day after my baby's birth, a social worker came bearing papers. I filled in the birth certificate with my name, my baby's name, and Chuck as father. I named my daughter Beryl Anne, not because I particularly liked the name, but because I knew someone named Beryl at the home. I didn't want to choose a name that would be too close to my heart. I signed the temporary placement papers, dressed my daughter, and we left the hospital—in different directions.

I returned to the home to recover for a couple of weeks. The social worker came to visit me again, and I signed the final papers. She shook my hand and wished me well. Following through with my mother's plan, I flew to Connecticut to visit the aunt I was supposed to have been staying with for those months. The story was that I was helping her take care of her new baby. I stayed with my aunt for about two weeks before returning home to my parents' house.

Everybody was so happy to have me back home again! My parents never spoke about the baby or the adoption. I built a sort of cement wall inside myself behind which I hid my feelings. I went into some kind of funk. I didn't know then what was going on, but it was like I wasn't quite all there—like a piece of me was missing. There was a terrible guilt—like I had become a second-class person unworthy of a good life. I have some knowledge now about what was happening to me, but I wish I had understood more then. It would have given me more control over what was to come.

After my "unfortunate break," as my parents referred to it, they decided to send me to secretarial school. I was still in a fog, probably clinically depressed. I went along with what they wanted, sort of dated and just floated along, with not much interest in anything or anyone. I muddled through school for a year. Then at age twenty, I started working for the government.

I began as a "GS-3" at the Department of the Interior and got an apartment with another girl. I had a terrible time being a secretary, but it wasn't for lack of trying. Anyone with a learning disability would recognize my problems, but I didn't know I had learning disabilities—or even what those were. My attention span was still bad, I had a hard time sitting still, and I couldn't remember the order in which to do things. I was great at dealing with complex problems, but I really messed up the simple tasks. Amazingly, I held that job for thirteen years.

In keeping with my "second-class" mentality, I settled for far less than the best. I picked the wrong friends, the wrong boyfriends, the wrong job—I even married the wrong man.

Through a mutual friend, I met Mark at a party. I could tell that he liked me right away, but he said we had to wait because he was entangled in a "marriage of convenience" to a very young girl who lived with his two-year-old baby in California.

We began dating anyway, and I was so impressed that someone actually wanted me that I never made a decision about what I wanted. Mark moved in with me after a few months. Our first big fight ended with me apologizing. This was the start of something bad. I apologized for everything, always trying to make things right. I should have stuck up for myself, but I just took all his guilty baggage along with my own, and when things got worse, I just worked harder to make it okay. But it was never okay.

Mark and I were married in April 1968 at Our Redeemer Lutheran Church—my church—in Falls Church, Virginia. I was twenty-four. We had a beautiful wedding and a boring honeymoon in St. Thomas. There wasn't anything to do, and we didn't enjoy each other's company all that much.

Mark was very moody—always running either hot or cold. I never knew what to expect. I tried to create a normal life for myself and went through the motions. On Wednesday evenings was choir practice, Saturday mornings laundry, and I got my hair done on Saturday afternoons. I handled the lawn and the garden, we shared the cooking and cleaning. I thought our life together, though dull, was tolerable. Our sex life was less than perfect. He never took time for my needs. Behind his back, I used to refer to him as "the rabbit." I really loved him, though.

Mark was upset about my never becoming pregnant. But I did become pregnant once. No one believed me at first when I said there was something wrong. The doctor put me on complete bed rest with pills for the pain and pills to help me sleep, but I lost the baby anyway. In fact, I almost died. It was an ectopic (tubal) pregnancy.

Apparently, Mark felt sorry enough for himself during that time to justify his having an affair. My parents couldn't even find him when they took me to the hospital. While I was fighting for my life, he was having sex with some other woman!

When I finally went home, I had lost forty pounds in three months and was terribly weak. Then the phone calls began. It was "Her," and she'd hang up if I answered. I knew I should leave Mark, but no one in my family had ever been divorced. I convinced myself that if I could just bear with it, things would somehow get better.

One time I even became forceful with him, delivering the ultimatum, "her or me." But we just went on as usual. I never got pregnant again. I thought about adoption. I had this feeling that since I had given up a child to adoption, I deserved another from someone else. Considering the two-year wait and the state of my marriage, I never pursued it aggressively.

Without consulting me, Mark applied for a job with the Baltimore Colts football team, which would involve moving and my having to change jobs. He was offered the job and accepted it before even notifying me. I found us a house in Baltimore and a moving company. My parents helped me get everything ready, and it was all moved in before Mark even saw the house.

I got a job as a secretary for Social Security. Mark continued to have affairs behind my back. I threatened to leave him for good if he didn't stop. Our relationship became more and more distant. It seemed to me that he had a confused view of reality, which was becoming a problem. He lost his job with the Colts, and then went on to a series of jobs, none of which he could hold for more than six months.

I started getting headaches from the pressure of working sixty to seventy hours a week in order to meet our financial obligations. Mark's typical day was watching television, taking care of the dog and puppies, smoking and drinking beer.

His drinking was also becoming a problem, but he said, "If it bothers you, then it's your problem."

Mark badgered and demeaned me in front of everyone. He made fun of me all the time. I found evidence of still another girlfriend, which he tried to deny. At that point, there seemed so little left of our marriage that I called the movers and my parents and had them pack me up and take me back home. Mark and I had been married for nine years at the time of our divorce.

I moved back to Virginia and lived with my parents. In spite of everything, I still loved Mark tremendously. But I knew he was going downhill, and I didn't want to go with him. He loved me too and told me so years later, after he had remarried. Our relationship was just too destructive. Breaking up was for the best.

It wasn't long before I had my own apartment. I began to travel, took scuba lessons and went on diving trips. I did almost anything to try to escape my real world. I tried drugs and drinking, but they didn't fill the void. I was real good at sex, but not good at intimacy. I had built a wall around myself and nobody was going to get in. I kept everyone at arm's length, including my family. I was not happy with this sort of life; I was just existing day to day.

I finally found out about my learning disabilities when I was in my mid-forties. Polly's son, my nephew, was being tested, and they said it ran in families—had anyone else been diagnosed? Neither my sister nor my brother-in-law had any symptoms. My sister shared all this information with me, which started me thinking.

I had just barely survived a performance review at work, with a less than outstanding rating because I "constantly mixed up phone numbers, forgot half the instructions given and forgot assignments." In tears, I called a school for people with learning disabilities and made an appointment to be tested. I figured it couldn't hurt.

At the appointment, I was diagnosed immediately with several learning disabilities. I remember sitting there and crying with relief. It was like a light suddenly went on in my life.

The director patiently explained what each disability meant in regard to how my world works. He explained that "LD" people don't learn or even think like other people do. He said that the tests also showed me to be near genius. He was amazed at the degree to which I had taught myself to learn. He said most people with such severe disabilities don't even make it through junior high school!

I was referred to a special eye doctor, who couldn't believe I worked with computers and graphics for a living. According to her tests, I don't really see. I'll never forget her words, "You must be made of piss and vinegar to have accomplished so much!"

It was the first time my accomplishments had ever been recognized, except by my mother. I was given special glasses and was astonished at the difference they made. No more headaches—no more awful eye strain.

Now a lot of things about my life made sense, including my insecurity and my inability to make decisions. I finally knew why everything had always been so hard for me!

I attended adult classes at the school for about two years. I tested at the college level in reading comprehension and math. My poor ego was certainly boosted by that!

A few years before my big discovery, I started attending a search/support group for women who had lost a child through adoption. I had visited the adoption agency, and they had provided all the standard non-identifying information. In fact, the social worker had left me alone in the room with the file folder. Being as naive as I was, it never occurred to me to peek.

Arlene

I didn't actively search for my daughter at first because of the walls I'd so painfully built, and because I didn't think I deserved the happiness of finding her. But after I found out about my learning disabilities, I knew that I needed to find her because of the possibility of her having inherited the LD monster. The growth and wisdom I was beginning to discover within myself helped me give myself permission to complete my search.

Since the adoption took place in Washington, D.C., where all the records are sealed, I found an underground "searcher" through another birth mother.

While they were outside gardening, I approached my parents about my decision to search for my daughter. "That's nice," my mother said, without looking up.

"What? What?" said my dad, who had become hard of hearing.

"She wants to find her daughter. You know, the adopted one."

Then they told me if I needed any money, nothing was too much. I should just let them know. They said that my daughter and I needed to find each other.

It was expensive. My parents just handed me the money—no questions asked. Within a day or two of my forwarding the money to the searcher, he called me to verify the information I already had. Two days later I got another call with complete information on my daughter. Her name was Linnea, and she lived in Kansas!

It was the beginning of a whole new life for me. It was, in a way, the beginning of my life. I was forty-seven, Linnea was twenty-nine. I called her for the first time on a January night, 1992. I had a pad of paper nearby so I could take notes.

"Is this Linnea Martinson?"

"Yes. Who is this?"

"My name is Arlene Griggs. Were you born on March 4th, 1962?"

"Yes."

"I had a baby on that day and placed her for adoption. I believe that you might be that baby."

She was crying. I was crying. I heard her husband in the background asking what was wrong.

"It's my mother," she replied. "My *real* mother."

I'll never forget how I felt, hearing those words. Her existence was a reality! We talked for a long time. I discovered that she had recently started searching for me! We made plans to talk again the next day, after she had time to digest everything.

It was like a honeymoon, only not boring this time. We exchanged letters, phone calls, photographs—she is so beautiful! I found out that I was a grandmother, too! We made plans for me to fly out to Kansas the following month and to share Linnea's thirtieth birthday with her and her family.

Linnea met me at the airport with an armful of flowers. There I was, forty-five pounds overweight, feeling ugly and worrying about what she'd think of me—and all she could do was grin! We had a great visit. And how can I describe the feeling of rocking my sweet baby grandson to sleep?

Linnea's adoptive mother was very supportive at first about us being reunited. Linnea's sister Diane also had been adopted and was in the process of looking for her biological roots, too. There were no other children in the family. The adoptive mother had been a medical technician, the father a high school teacher. At the time of Linnea's adoption, they lived in northern Virginia—about a quarter mile from my parents' home! The father taught in the very high school my sister attended! When Linnea was about four, her adoptive father had returned to school and had become a Lutheran minister. Until his health failed, the family had moved from state to state to serve various congregations. A heavy smoker, her father developed heart trouble and died when Linnea was a senior in high school.

I flew Linnea and the baby back to Virginia for my parents' fiftieth wedding anniversary party. It was a boisterous, happy house full of friends and relatives, which smoothed over the announcement of "Oh, by the way, Arlene had a baby, placed her for adoption, and here she is."

Virtually no one had known about Linnea, but everyone seemed happy. My sister Polly took my hand and said, "Now this is the Arlene I used to know. There's a joy about you now—no more sadness."

I've been smiling ever since I found my daughter. She is a lot like me—intellectually inquiring and physically active. She loved it when they lived in Oklahoma, where she was a cheerleader for her high school wrestling team.

Arlene

The entire birth mother family

Before moving to Kansas, she attended college in Oklahoma and met her future husband there.

Linnea's adoptive mother seemed very interested in all the similarities of our families at first, but her interest seemed to cool after we met. Some time in 1994, my relationship with my daughter started to change. After being so close and involved in each other's lives, Linnea informed me that her mother was very insecure about our relationship.

"She is uneasy about 'us' and doesn't want to hear about 'us' any more," Linnea said, hesitantly.

I know she didn't want to hurt my feelings. After that our phone conversations became strained, and she became more and more distant. I wrote to my daughter, letting her know that I didn't like things this way but that I would accept anything she felt she needed to do. I did not receive a reply.

Mom says I'll hear from her again after her adoptive mother dies. I really don't like the idea of waiting around for someone to die, but there's nothing I can do about the situation. At Christmas I sent a family-type gift to

Linnea, her husband, and my grandson. Every March I send a huge bouquet
of flowers with a card that reads, "Happy Birthday. Love, Arlene."

I have a good career as secretary to three officers at the Federal Reserve
Board. My work with graphics remains fascinating to me. I test new software
programs and teach classes about how to use them. Imagine! Me—the learning disabled one—teaching others!

No matter what happens, my entire life has changed because of finding
my daughter. I am a whole person again. To this day, though, I cannot believe
that I allowed my parents and pastor to take my child away. I can't alter what
was, and I have very little control over the future, but at least I am no longer
in the dark. I feel good about myself now, and am no longer ashamed of having had a baby. I have lost weight and look forward to the future.

I am making real plans about the rest of my life, rather than going
through the fog, day by day.

My sister Polly and I are very close now. I may even retire in California
where she is living, so we can be together. As for my folks, Dad has become
very religious and thoughtful of others. He remembers all the details that Mom
now forgets. They are a perfect team, and their roles have adjusted with age.
Dad is the one who keeps in contact with everybody—calling or writing if he
hasn't heard from us in a while.

I love music, theater, movies, and my dog, Bruno. I even love to read,
although I'm very slow at it. My activities are a little less combative than they
used to be, but I still dive, ride bike and do some aerobics and weight training.
I enjoy potting, when I have access to a wheel and kiln. And I'm still my mother's daughter—I still love to cook. I have assisted chefs at a professional cooking school and may go to chef's school when I retire.

I don't have the relationship with my daughter that I want to have—that
I did have for almost two years. But I still feel that we are connected. I feel it
in my soul that we will be reunited again some day. This all has been unbelievably painful for me to remember. My fondest wish is that Linnea will soon
open the door again and say, "Come on in."

But for now, I have found her, and that needs to be enough.

* * *

Chapter Four

ೞ *Karla* ೞ

Only child, lonely child. That was me growing up. In 1939, when I was three, my mother divorced my father and sent me to live with her parents on the family farm in northern Minnesota. I don't think Mom ever knew how abandoned and unloved I would feel—as a little kid and for the rest of my life. My mother had her own problems. I didn't realize it then, but she was an alcoholic, destined to marry an unfortunate succession of alcoholic and abusive husbands.

I only remember nighttime things about my father. I remember watching his big white shoes glowing in the dark as he stepped heavily across our linoleum floor. And I remember one night when he was drinking and hitting Mom, I protested. He pushed me out the window and I fell onto the fire escape and huddled there for hours, afraid to go back into the apartment. It was cold. I remember thinking, "Why doesn't Mom fight back?" But she never did.

Living with my grandparents was hard work. My grandparents were very poor and very strict. Their motto was, "If you don't work you don't eat." Even as a little child I had to feed the chickens, peel potatoes, scrub my grandfather's dirty socks and more. I really didn't mind the work. I think the highly structured environment was good for me. I knew what to expect, and I knew my limits.

My grandparents didn't own a tractor, let alone a car. Gramp had built the two-room log cabin with his own hands, and farmed with a team of horses. They were pious Methodists who lived by the rule, "Spare the rod, spoil the child."

The grandparents

Every day I'd get up at 4:00 A.M., do barn chores and house chores, then walk three and one-half miles to Spring Creek School. It was a one-room schoolhouse. My teacher, Mrs. Hutchinson, taught the eight-student class that spanned five grades.

After school, I'd help prepare the evening meal. When the crops were bad, we ate mush— a mixture of flour and milk. Gram tried to fix it all sorts of different ways, sometimes mixing pota- toes into it. After supper we listened to the radio for a while, read the Bible, then went to bed.

We got drinking water from the river and kept it in a pail. We saved rainwater to wash our hair. Milk and cheese came from our two cows. I still remember the day one of them died. It was terrible. When a family has only two cows and loses one of them, that's traumatic.

Perishable food was kept in crocks sunken into the cool ground and tightly covered, so snakes wouldn't get in. On winter nights, we had to keep an all-night vigil at the wood stove so the water in the house wouldn't freeze.

Gram washed our clothes in two tin tubs. She'd boil the clothes first on the stove and then scrub them on the washboard. Sometimes her knuckles would bleed. She never complained.

Karla

On weekends Gram instructed me in sewing and baking, and sometimes Gramp would take me fishing. I loved going fishing with Gramp, watching the sun sparkle on the river. It made me feel special, being together with him. Peaceful, too.

Every so often my mother showed up at the farmhouse door, wanting me to come live with her again. So off I'd go, with my sad little suitcase and big expectations. My hopes for a happy family never lasted long though, and I'd usually be back with my grandparents within a few weeks. Mom said it was because her job as a waitress took up so much time. I knew that she had boyfriends, too, and was "sick" a lot.

I saw Gram and Gramp as perfect people. I still do. They were my protectors. I always tried hard to please them. I know my grandparents loved me in their own way, but I couldn't seem to overcome the empty feeling of loneliness I always carried around inside me. At night in my bed, I watched the stars through my window and dreamed about growing up, marrying someone who really loved me and having twelve beautiful children. We'd be a real family. I could almost see their rosy little faces.

My mother remarried in 1949 when I was thirteen. She sent a letter to Gram wondering if I wanted to come live with them in Minneapolis. I was ecstatic. Finally, we could be a family! I begged Gram to let me go. I think she knew it wasn't a good idea, but she helped me pack and paid my train fare. The neighbor drove me to the train station. I can still remember Gram and Gramp, looking so sorry, standing at the rickety back door of the farmhouse.

I guess Mom didn't remember that I was coming. I ended up waiting on the apartment steps until the bars closed. I'll never forget the look of shock on my stepfather's face when he saw me there. She hadn't even told him that I existed! That made two surprises because I couldn't help but notice that my mother was pregnant. I felt like Mom had betrayed me, and I'll bet my stepfather felt betrayed too.

Ours was not a happy household. There was a lot of yelling and fighting. There was mental and physical abuse and, of course, alcoholism. I remember books being thrown, dishes being broken, a lot of swearing and feeling like I wanted to disappear. My grandparents had taught me about God and right from wrong, but there was no religion in my mother's house. I was so confused.

53

Shadow Mothers

At school I fell in with a rowdy crowd, which by today's standards would be considered tame. I chose them as friends because they were the only kids who accepted me. We'd go to the drive-ins for Cokes and fries and to the park where Jerry played guitar and we all sang along. Some of the kids smoked cigarettes, but not me. I was always at someone else's place or hanging out somewhere. Because I was so embarrassed by my family, I never brought a friend to my house.

When my little half sister, Leah, was born, I became the instant built-in baby sitter. More than a baby sitter, actually—I was more like her mother. It felt good to me, doing something important like taking care of a baby. Little children don't hurt you like adults can. But I had to take her with me wherever I went, and that was a pain. If only my mother had kept a better eye on things, she would have realized this was too much responsibility for a fourteen-year old.

Once when Leah was still a baby, I stayed out all night with my friends from school. It was completely innocent. We just listened to records and had Cokes. But when I came home, Mom shouted at me about what a tramp I was and dragged me to the doctor to be "checked." I don't think she believed the doctor when he assured her my virginity was still intact. It may sound strange, but I still feel hurt that she didn't believe me. And that doctor visit was so embarrassing!

At fifteen, I started running away from home. I just had to get out of there. I felt that if I stayed in that sick place any longer, I would explode. But they always found me and brought me back. My stepfather didn't have a clue about how to handle kids, let alone a teenager. My mother kept telling me, "If you don't do something right, you'll never amount to anything!" But instead of trying harder, I began losing what little confidence I had in myself.

In spite of my outward behavior, I still believed in the strict morals my grandparents had taught me. I was truly appalled when I found out about "bad girls." Although sex was an unmentionable subject, especially in my grandparents' home, I firmly believed that to have sex before marriage was a terrible sin.

On the farm, whenever I'd been scolded or felt unhappy, I had my own special "magic" place—a clearing in the woods where the trees grew together at the top like a church steeple. I would stand there, on top of a stump, and

54

sing "Mockingbird Hill" as loud as I could. The leaves moved and rustled against each other as if they were applauding, and I bowed to my appreciative audience, yearning to become a real singer someday.

There was no place to sing at my Mom's house. I couldn't stand my life —never knowing who would be drunk or who would throw things. Maybe I kept running away to get attention. Negative attention was better than nothing. My mom and stepdad started turning me in to the police, and I found myself in the juvenile court system.

I knew I wasn't a bad girl, but I felt like I couldn't figure out anything, except that everything was my fault. The one thing that made sense to me was when a judge said, "This girl doesn't belong here. And the next time you people are back here in court, you will be the ones that I'll punish."

At seventeen, I met Charlie, who was in the navy. I fell for him like a ton of bricks—his brown curly hair, cute smile, and handsome uniform. I felt extremely guilty about having sex with him, but since I gave him my virginity I knew I had to give him my hand.

We got married that same year—1953. It was a small, quiet wedding. We moved in with his brother in Michigan. It was hard, having to live with another couple. Charlie was always nice enough, but he never wanted to get a job. My grandparents brought me up to believe that a husband was supposed to support his wife. I wanted to make something of my marriage, but Charlie just couldn't change.

I divorced him when I was eighteen and moved back to Minneapolis, where I worked as a waitress during the day and as a ballroom dance teacher at night. The dance school trained me. My real father had been a musician, so maybe that's why I've always loved music. I shared a little apartment with another girl and life seemed tolerable, even happy sometimes. I even got myself a job as a cocktail lounge singer, which was a dream come true.

Then Tim came into my life, with his flashing smile and coal-black eyes. Tim was wonderful, loved to dance, and drank only 7-Up. The only problem was, Tim was still married. But his wife didn't understand him, and they were separated. Yes, I was pretty dumb.

Believing he'd soon be free, I let myself get carried away, and in 1955, at the ripe old age of nineteen, I found myself pregnant and unmarried. What's worse,

Karla, 1953

when Tim's wife found out he was seeing somebody, she wanted him back. He was like a ping pong ball between the two of us. He said it was the pressure that started him drinking again. I didn't even know he had a drinking problem! I didn't want any more drunks in my life, but I was stuck. I loved him.

I continued singing as long as I could—mostly one-nighters. One of the bands with whom I sang wanted me just to sit there on stage and look pretty. I joined a trio and went country, which was more stable than pop. Our gigs were all over the five-state area, from Bismarck, North Dakota, to Brainerd, Minnesota, to Iowa City, Iowa.

I couldn't sing or work in public after I started showing, so I baby-sat for neighbors until Mary was born. When I looked into her sweet little face for the first time, I thought to myself, "That's it for me. Now I will always be one of those 'bad' girls." But I loved my baby daughter fiercely and was determined to escape from my past.

Karla

I scraped up enough money to take a train to Los Angeles, California, where I found a job in a pastrami shop, a cheap apartment, and a baby sitter for Mary. I never let Tim know where we were because I knew I had to get over him.

For several months everything was settled and peaceful. Then, another uniform entered the picture. At first I thought Rollie was a police officer, but it turned out he was just a security guard. We had a lot in common, with both of us being Norwegian and from the Midwest. He took me out to dinner and dancing, and never seemed to drink too much. It was good to have a little fun again.

One day I got a letter from Mom. Because of a big fight with my stepdad, she wanted to bring my half sister Leah to Los Angeles and stay with me. What could I do? I gave up my apartment, rented a bigger one than I could afford, and tried to prepare myself for living with Mom again.

Mom and Leah were only with me a couple of weeks before Mom patched things up with my stepdad. I should never have let it happen, but Mom talked me into letting her take Mary home with her. I was so dumb. I knew my finances were a mess, and figured I'd work two jobs, get ahead and then send for Mary. Rollie thought it was a good idea, and I went along with it.

After Mom left with Leah and my daughter, Rollie and I moved in together. As luck would have it, Rollie had a drinking problem too. I ignored it for as long as I could. But I was starting to feel lost and lonely again, and missed my baby terribly. I remember watching the neighborhood children out the window. The sound of their playing and laughing became louder and louder, until it was a roaring in my head. At that point something snapped, and I knew I just had to have my sweet daughter back with me.

Rollie was hurt when I left. He believed I was going back to Tim, no matter how I tried to convince him otherwise. Ignoring Rollie's protests, I sold everything I owned, which was barely enough for the round trip train fare to Minnesota.

I arrived in Minneapolis only to discover that Tim's mother had taken Mary to Texas. My own mother hadn't even informed me! Barely able to think, I exchanged my return ticket to California for a ticket to Houston.

I'm not a brave person, and I don't know how I had the guts, but I made the cab wait in front of Tim's mother's house, ran in, grabbed my baby, and left in the same cab. Tim's mother was so shocked, she didn't even protest. It was pretty dramatic, like something out of a soap opera. But I had my Mary, and I promised my little girl we would never be separated again.

Back in Minneapolis and totally broke, I called Rollie and asked him for money for Mary and me to come home. "Don't bother coming back," was what he told me.

He assumed I had gotten together with Tim, and it hadn't worked out. I could tell by his voice that Rollie had been drinking. But I didn't think I had a choice. I had to go back to California because I was pregnant with Rollie's baby. I thought I belonged with him, and was sure I could convince Rollie to take me back. We could get married and be a family.

Isn't it funny that, after everything, I had such a positive attitude? Like Mary Poppins, I always believed in a bright side. Maybe that's part of what makes me a survivor.

I begged Mom for some money to get to California, and she finally gave it to me. Nobody knew I was pregnant. Not Mom, not my grandparents—nobody except Rollie, who was cold as stone and flatly refused to see me. I was more lonely than ever, depressed and scared. I cried all the time. I couldn't understand how Rollie could turn his back on me.

Feeling desperate, I went to the Red Cross in Los Angeles. They were kind and helped me find a baby sitter for Mary so I could work. They also put me in touch with a California adoption agency. The agency social worker explained adoption and offered to help me find a place to live and pay my medical bills, but only if I would agree to the unselfish act of giving up my child to a loving couple unable to have children.

According to the social worker, the only clients this agency had were loving, well-established and able to give my baby everything I couldn't. It was made clear to me that this would be in the best interest of my unborn child. Miserable, I agreed. There really was no other choice.

Shortly after my signing up with the agency, Mary and I moved in with a rich family in Sherman Oaks. I cooked, cleaned and took care of their children in return for a room where I could occasionally escape. I was so lonely and sad, knowing there was much more sadness up ahead. I felt like I was drowning, but I had to put on a happy face for my employer and for Mary. I'm sure that kind of stress takes its toll on a person's health.

I became very sick with the Asian flu, had a high fever and drifted in and out of consciousness. Weak as a kitten, I went into labor two weeks early. The lady who had given me a job took me to the hospital and left me there. She was nice enough to take care of Mary while I was gone. It was a very long and difficult delivery and a breach birth. I was pretty much out of it, but after I woke up, I begged to see my new baby girl. The nurses weren't going to allow it at first, but they couldn't calm me any other way. I had to know she was perfect so she'd get a good family.

My baby and I spent little pieces of time together each day. I named her Constance. I knew this was my only chance to ever talk to her so I told her, "Always be a good girl, honey. And remember, Mommy will love you forever."

One day the adoption agency social worker walked in while I was holding Constance. She was so angry! I'll never forget the feeling of her pulling my baby out of my arms.

When the social worker handed me the papers, I couldn't see where to sign my name because of the tears. It was hard to breathe. There was such a deep pain inside me. But I signed, feeling great pressure to keep my word to the adoption agency. I was never told I could change my mind. I was never told there might have been a way for me to keep Constance, such as getting help from welfare. I was made to understand that once I signed the papers, that was it. No waiting period. No going back.

Nobody knew I had given birth to another daughter, so I had no support system at all. The sadness, sickness, and loneliness had left me thin and pale. It was all I could do to take care of Mary.

For the next month, I was in deep depression. I didn't want to see anyone, but when Mary's father, Tim, called from out of the blue, I agreed to have dinner with him. He told me that he was finally divorced, had quit drinking and was in California to tell me that now we could get married. I thought, "Oh, why couldn't this have happened a month ago?"

I told Tim about the baby, and he was sympathetic. It was nice being with someone who understood me.

Tim and I did marry. I began looking for information about my baby when Constance was about three months old. The adoption agency acted as if I didn't exist. The following year I gave birth to another daughter, who only lived two days because her lungs weren't fully developed. We moved back to Minnesota, and I became pregnant again, but there was something wrong, and the doctors had to abort my baby son. They told me I could never have any more children. I figured this was my punishment for all my sins.

Every few months I wrote to California, asking the agency for news about Constance. Those first letters were never answered.

During our seven years of marriage, Tim fought an uphill battle with his alcoholism. Our relationship became more and more strained. I finally gave up, and we divorced.

I tried again to find Constance, but the adoption agency still would not return my phone calls. When I finally did get to talk to a real person, I was refused any information. I dedicated myself to raising Mary and trying to keep my head on straight. Mary was a beautiful child with a sweet disposition and very talented musically. I worked hard to make sure I could always afford her dance lessons, which she loved.

In 1963, while working as a waitress in a bar, I met Len, the bar manager. We dated for several months, and he appeared to be a hard worker and very mature. It was only after we were married that I discovered that he had problems not only with alcohol but also with other women.

I became pregnant almost right away. Len became physically and verbally abusive. He didn't think I was "his" anymore if I was carrying a child. I think it had something to do with the hatred he had for his mother that he transferred to me. I told Len we had to go to marriage counseling but he said, "No way. I'm not telling any stranger about my private life."

In spite of everything, I had two children with him. Theresa and John were both "miracle babies," both premature. Theresa weighed less than two pounds, John just over three pounds. God blessed me with the gift of them, and they both overcame all the physical problems associated with early birth.

Karla

After seven years of marriage to Len, I decided I didn't want my kids to live like that and didn't want them to see Len hit me anymore. Above all, I didn't want to be like Mom and not fight back. Hence, my third divorce.

I stepped up my efforts to find Constance. In my mind, if I could just find her, I would feel whole again. As I mentioned, during the first ten years of searching, my requests to the agency were ignored. I went to libraries and looked for clues from all over the country. During the second decade the agency began answering my letters but told me no information was available. I kept searching through any records I could find.

For the third ten years, I searched like a woman possessed. The urge to find her became stronger and stronger until it was the biggest thing in my life. Now I was writing weekly letters to the agency, pleading for information. Every lunch hour, every evening, every weekend found me in the library checking all sorts of records, including California telephone books.

My other three children were growing up, and I tried hard to take care of their needs. But every night when I went to bed, when everything was quiet, I felt like my lost baby was calling out for me.

The Mormon Library was very helpful to me in searching the birth records of Los Angeles County. When I knew Constance was old enough to be married, I began checking Los Angeles County marriage records.

During this period of time, I changed the way I was praying. Instead of praying so hard that God would let me find her, I began praying for her—for her soul and her health.

Finally in 1990, I located someone I thought might be my daughter. Something inside me told me this was my daughter. I could hardly believe it. After wasting so much time looking in other parts of the country, there she was in Los Angeles—right where I had left her!

I gathered every bit of information I could about her, including address and phone number. But something stopped me from making the call. I couldn't do it. I couldn't face the possibility of being rejected again. It took me three months to get up the courage to dial that long distance phone number. I can't say how often I picked up the phone and put it back down again.

The night I actually did call, I made notes of all the things I wanted to say to her and arranged them around the phone. I must have rehearsed everything a hundred times. This was the toughest performance I had ever prepared. I was scared of doing something wrong or forgetting something. I was just plain terrified.

She answered the phone. I said quickly, "First thing, I want to give you my name and number," thinking she might hang up on me.

Then I asked her if her birth date was July 12, 1957. She said yes. I asked if the name Constance meant anything to her, and she said yes, her birth mother had given her that name, but of course it had been changed.

Then she said, "Are you my mother?"

I said, "I believe I am."

It's funny but I don't even remember what we said next, but we talked that night for an hour, and another hour the next night. We both cried a lot. She started calling me "Mom" right away.

Unfortunately, because I am an expert on the subject, I soon was able to tell that my birth daughter, Liz, had been a victim of abuse. She started confiding in me immediately with a trust that usually takes a long time to build.

Liz

As it turned out, her brother had sexually abused her for years. This was so ironic and horrible for me. I thought placing her for adoption would guarantee her a better life. She hadn't gone to college either, and that was another thing I had been promised.

Her adoptive mother was very negative about our meeting. She was in the beginning stages of Alzheimer's then and soon could remember nothing, so we'll never know much about her feelings. Her adoptive dad thought it was great that Liz and I had found each other after all these years. He told me little stories about when she was growing up, showed me family photo albums and always treated me with kindness.

My other children, all grown up by then, were very accepting of Liz. We all went to the airport to meet her for the first time, and my children took turns hugging her. I think they were happy for me and relieved that their mother didn't have to search any more.

My daughter Theresa, soft and tender as ever, said, "It's about time something good like this happened to Mom."

I felt like the circle of my life was made whole again. Every day I still pray in thanksgiving for the incredible gift of my birth daughter.

Another irony is that my birth daughter was in the process of a divorce when I first met her. Her husband was an alcoholic, and he physically abused her. They had a thirteen-year-old son, Tad, which made me an instant grandmother. At every possible chance, Liz and Tad came to visit, or we flew to California to visit them. Our relationship became closer and closer.

Liz is the only one of my children who asks my advice—and actually takes it! And of all my children, she is the one who looks most like me. I feel strongly that she has always needed me—and I've always needed her. Now that we're together, we cling to each other like glue.

At her request, I located Rollie, so she could know her birth father and have complete answers about nationality and health issues. He and his wife of twenty years were elated to meet Liz. They hadn't been able to have any children together.

I was happy that it worked out so well and thrilled to learn that Rollie had been dry for ten years. Birth father and daughter have formed a special bond and live only two hours apart from each other. Liz thanked me for finding her birth father and says it makes her feel more complete.

Since Liz and I met, she has remarried and had another son, Teddy. I'm just as crazy about these two boys as I am about my other grandchildren—six in all, plus one great grandchild!

Because Tad doesn't get along with his stepfather very well, he came to Minneapolis to live with me. We're so proud of him because he graduated from high school in 1998. Liz, Teddy, and her husband joined us for a big graduation picnic in Tad's honor. He has a job now, and has a very sweet girlfriend. I would like him to continue school, but that will have to be Tad's decision. He definitely doesn't want to go back to California, though. Mary's daughter, my granddaughter Catherine, and her baby Sherrie, my great-granddaughter, also live with me, along with my cat and dog. It's a nice big family, much like the daydream I used to have when I was little.

I look back at all those years of searching and frustration, and I can't really say it was worth it, because certain things should never happen to anyone. I probably could have benefited from counseling, but I didn't know there was anything out of the ordinary about my life. And counseling wasn't always available in those days.

The feeling of abandonment—that everyone would leave me for someone or something else—was constant. Even now, I still have to fight against those feelings.

Every year around Liz's birthday, I used to become physically sick, sometimes bedridden. Since I found her, I am calmer and more at peace. I've even stopped biting my nails. I am thrilled that I have a happy ending to talk about.

Above all, the entire experience of Liz has served to strengthen my faith. Once I gave up the "me" part in my prayers, God seemed to open the door and allow to find my birth daughter. I've heard that God makes the cake and lets us add the finishing touches. In my case, I started with a big and confusing bunch of ingredients—but ended up with a wonderfully decorated cake!

* * *

Chapter Five

✺ *Bette* ✻

I was sick a lot when I was a kid and completely wrapped up in my own little world, as children sometimes are. I was boisterous and outgoing. "Don't be so loud!" was probably the phrase I heard most often.

People said I looked just like Elizabeth Taylor, and I believed them. I loved pretending that I was a star, and once staged a circus for charity in a vacant lot with my friends and my wonder-dog, Chips. People actually came! We made a lot of money and sent it to the Damon Runyon Foundation, an organization for helping sick children. The Foundation even sent us a thank you note.

Our extended family and everyone we knew lived nearby. Our neighborhood in the late 1940s and early 1950s was like a small town, although it was part of New York City. Surrounded by caring aunts, uncles, cousins, family friends, and my big sister, Alicia Jo, who looked like Grace Kelly, I was confident of my place in the world.

Except when my dad was out of town on one of his many business trips. Then I was desolate. I'd get stomach aches so bad that Mom would have to take me to Dr. Cohen, who thought that my mom should try to find someone who could act as a surrogate dad for me. Mom asked Mr. Melvin, who tried his best, letting me sit in his lap and making a fuss over me. I don't think he was very comfortable in the role, though, and neither was I. I think Mr. Melvin's daughter resented it, too, so we gave it up. The stomach aches eventually went away but not until I was an adult.

I remember when Dad used to let my sister and me comb his hair into ridiculous styles while he'd make a funny face to heighten the effect. And I remember us climbing onto Mom and Dad's big bed on Saturday mornings to wake him up for breakfast, with the sweet smell of bacon wafting from the kitchen.

Mom was a nurse and worked full time, but in my memory she was always there. She took Alicia Jo and me to the pool on hot summer days, and when we couldn't use the public pool because of the polio epidemic, she set up the lawn sprinkler in the yard for us. I remember exactly how she smelled in her satin gown when she kissed us good night before she and Dad went out to the Masonic Hall. It was a heady combination of cigarettes, Tabu perfume, and Clorets.

One of my best childhood memories is when I discovered that my sister liked me. Alicia Jo was the smartest person on the planet and three years older than I was. I figured she hated me because she always ditched me when I tried to play with her. But when I became very sick with encephalitis and needed to be taken to the hospital, she sat with me for hours. She told me little stories and played little games to try to keep me awake because they didn't want me to go into a coma before Dr. Cohen got there. After that, no matter what happened between us, I always knew that she really cared about me.

My whole life changed when we moved from New York to a town just west of Minneapolis. I was ten, and we knew only a few people—some of Mom's relatives. There weren't any Angellinis, Picarellos, or Cohens, either. Everybody was blonde as lutefisk and had absolutely no accent.

I didn't fit in—the way I looked (I was short and round with black hair), the way I talked (I had a lisp in addition to the New York accent), and the way I acted (loud and obnoxious). I had zero friends. I did have my Arthur Godfrey guitar though, and I could sing pretty well. I guess I acted the way I did to get attention, but it never really worked the way I wanted.

In junior high school, I met Kay. She was loud like me, beautiful, talented and funny. We were a striking pair—Kay was as blonde as I was dark. She thought I was beautiful and funny, too. We shared a rather strange sense of humor, joking about almost everything, including her father's accidental death in the basement of her home, and the fact that she was adopted. We spent all our free time together—usually at her house.

Kay lived with her mother and older brother, and together we listened to classical music and discussed subjects like history and politics. At home, if I tried to state an opinion about grown-up subjects like that, Dad would tell me, "You're not old enough to have an opinion," and, "When I want to hear what you think, I'll let you know."

But at Kay's house, my opinion and input were always welcomed.

I worked very hard at trying to fit in at school. I tried out for the cheerleading team and made it! Kay never seemed to worry about fitting in. We joined the Thespian Club together and got some meaty roles because of our acting talents. We were inseparable.

By the time I was a junior, I was starting to believe that I fit in just fine when I really wanted. Unfortunately, that positive sense of self was short lived.

Will, a senior, came from New York like me. His family was wealthy, interesting and well-educated, and their house was full of art. His mom was an artist and a poet. I wanted an artistic life like theirs. Will played football but had kind of an aloof attitude with the other kids. He was a very cool guy and listened to jazz.

As it turns out, Will was not a nice boy. He didn't tell me that he already had a girlfriend and only wanted me for sex. I thought we were going steady and desperately wanted to please him. After the first time we had sex, Will told me I was not very good at it and that I should get some experience and come back and see him when I knew what I was doing. Maybe that's why I spent the next few months having sex with anyone who would have me. Or maybe it was because I wanted someone to love me, even if it was just for five minutes.

Kay was having sex with a lot of guys too, and she always made a big joke out of it. When she suggested a competition to see which of us could have sex with the most guys that summer, the race was on! I had become that dreaded word, a slut. I remember getting ready to leave for a party and Dad telling me to go back upstairs and scrub my face. "You look like a French whore," he said.

Many years later, I learned that my deep need for reassurance caused me to somehow punish myself with my own sexuality. The result was a growing sense of self-loathing.

I went to Zion Lutheran Church every Sunday with Mom and my sister, while Dad took his Sunday morning bath. He had always been very active in our old congregation, but he never set foot in a church after we left Staten Island. I wasn't sure why.

Bette and her mother

During my senior year, I met Al, who said he loved me in spite of everything I had done. Al was a Baptist who promised to save me from myself. After graduation, I started at the University of Minnesota with Kay, just as we had always planned. But for some reason, nothing felt real. I'd come home on weekends and pretend everything was fine, but nothing was fine. Dad had a girlfriend, and my sister and I knew it. I think my mother knew, but she was pretending that everything was fine, too.

Al worked at a gas station, didn't want a college education and didn't think I should have one either. Especially if we were to be married. I convinced myself that marrying Al would make everything okay. I remember our Lutheran minister coming to the house the night before I was to be married, trying to talk me out of this "terrible mistake." He said I would be damning my unborn children to hell because Baptists don't baptize infants. As it turned out, I had no children in that marriage, so no souls were at risk. Except my own.

It was a huge wedding with a beautiful white gown and hundreds of guests. We spent money my parents didn't have—and just in time for Dad to walk me down the aisle before leaving Mom for a younger woman.

Al abused me physically, worked me like a slave and ran around with other women. We were managing a moderately priced motel. I did all the laundry, supervised the cafe and handled the books. My health began to suffer, and the doctor said I should leave my husband if he wouldn't let me rest more. When I told Al I wanted to leave, he advised me that I'd be leaving God, not just the marriage, and that staying married to him was my only chance at salvation. Lonely and desperate, I had an affair with Rick, the night manager, who was college educated and sympathized with me about how bad things were with Al. He also thought I was smart.

Bette

When I finally got up the courage to leave Al, I approached Mom for a place to stay. Mom had her own problems trying to make a life for herself without Dad. Kay knew everything about what had been going on. She and her mother offered to take me in until my mom could handle my coming home, which ended up being only a short time.

That was a good time for Mom and me, Chips, and my cat, Sam. I got a job at the hospital where Mom was a nurse, and we drove to work together every day. We were pretty broke and awfully sad, but we shared it all together.

Unfortunately my judgment hadn't improved, and I kept letting men mess up the picture. I fell in love with Rick, but I was still married to Al; Rick was still married, too, and still living with his wife. It was all very tawdry, but I put a great deal of energy into making everything work out. Kay knew about all of this and kept trying to introduce me to younger, more eligible guys. She'd invite me to parties and set up double dates, and I'd go, telling lies to Rick along the way.

One night at a party, Kay ran into a guy she wanted to be with, and I said I'd be able to get a ride home. A guy named Bill was all too glad to take me home. He just had to stop by his house on the way to pick up something. And would I just run in with him for a minute? He did take me home—several hours later.

That morning in my own bed, I knew what happened, but I didn't remember details. I couldn't remember drinking enough to explain the loss of memory, either. I discovered I was pregnant about a month later. I wasn't positive if Bill was the father or if it was Rick, but it was probably Rick.

I went into hiding. We didn't let anyone know—not my dad, not even my sister at first. Just Mom, Rick, Kay, and I were in on it. From the very beginning, I knew that this baby would be adopted by someone who could give him a good future. The best thing I could do was to hide my pregnancy and make sure the family in New York never knew, to spare my mother the shame. I thought I would pick up my life again after the baby was born—that my life would continue as if it never happened. After all, that's exactly what Kay had done the year before, and she seemed to be fine, still laughing and joking as usual. Kay would be there to help me through it all.

Rick and I rented an apartment on the outskirts of Minneapolis where we didn't know anybody. My cat and I lived there, and Rick stayed there sometimes. Mom brought me groceries and spent time with me when she could, but I could see how disappointed she was in me.

The other people in the apartment building thought my husband worked out of town. They were very kind to me and even surprised me with a baby shower—which, of course, was the last thing I wanted.

When Rick could get away from his wife he would come for me, and I would lie on the floor of the car so I wouldn't be seen on the way to the drive-in movie. Those movies were the only times I would leave the apartment. Kay stopped by often to play cribbage, make popcorn and watch TV with me. Our friendship was the most important part of my life.

I was eight months pregnant when Kay was killed. She had just turned twenty-one and was the victim of a head-on collision with a drunk driver. I was told that she probably died quickly and didn't suffer. I couldn't go to her funeral because I was still in hiding. I remember long nights at my window, watching the distant lights of the airport on the endless black horizon.

When my labor pains started, Rick drove me to the big new hospital on the south side of town. Mom met us there, and all the good things I remember about that day have to do with Mom. She was my guardian, defender, private-duty nurse, and advocate. Mine was going to be one of the first babies born at that hospital, and the staff was planning to make a big to-do about it—until they realized my circumstances.

When it was time to take me to the delivery room, the nurse who was taking care of me said sarcastically, "Great! This is just what I needed right now!"

After my son was born, I asked to count his fingers and toes and make sure his body was normal. I had heard that people did not adopt babies who were not perfect. If there had been something wrong with him I would have kept him rather than let him spend his life in an institution. He was perfect. I let them take him away, knowing I would never see him again. I didn't let myself feel very much emotion. I wanted everything to be over. Years later I thought I must have been the coldest person in the world, but it was all I could do then. Maybe I was protecting myself.

Bette

I was placed in a double room with a married woman who had her baby and her happy family with her often. The contrast between her happiness and my emptiness was too difficult for me, and Mom managed to come up with the extra money for a private room.

A social worker came to see me, tried to convince me to hold my baby one more time and reconsider my decision to place him for adoption. Now that I look back on it, I'm sure she simply wanted to be sure I had made a well-considered decision, but at the time I thought she was being judgmental. Besides, I never did really make a decision. Giving him up was all I could do. It was what Rick wanted and what Mom needed me to do. I didn't hold my son again.

I went back to the apartment and told the people there that my baby had died. It was awful to have to keep lying, but it seemed so important at the time to protect the secret. I returned all the lovely baby gifts they had given me, endured their condolences and recuperated for a few weeks. I hated myself by then—not so much for giving up my baby, but for all the lies. I never really allowed myself to feel the loss of my baby until years later.

When the legal papers were ready, I signed them. Rick agreed to be named as father so the baby could be adopted without my husband ever knowing. Then it was all over. My baby was really gone.

After our divorces were final, Rick and I got married. We built a home and I got pregnant. Weeks passed, and the very day we signed the loan closing papers for our house, I lost the baby. The doctors said I would probably never carry a baby full term. We kept trying, but every pregnancy ended in miscarriage. I had known there would be a price to pay and this was my punishment. I would never be allowed another child.

Our big beautiful house was full of empty rooms. We looked into adoption and even went through the initial interviews. I figured it would be an even exchange—that I deserved someone else's child since someone else had mine. But we found out that there was a two-year waiting period and just never pursued it further.

Circumstances eventually brought children into our household. I happily welcomed Derek and Robbie, who were four and seven. Their dad, Rick's brother, had divorced his wife and moved to Saigon to run a bar for GIs—and the kids needed a home. He wouldn't let his ex-wife have them and didn't want them with him in Vietnam. But I sure wanted them.

Rick and I tried to build a life for these children and ourselves. We got involved in our community with Little League and children's choir. Rick ran for city council, and I joined a community education group that evolved into a civil rights organization. I had quit my clerking job at the insurance company to spend more time with the boys, but when Rick's business failed, it was clear I needed to work again. Through our political contacts, I found a job as bookkeeper for the state of Minnesota with a drunk driving prevention program.

Eventually my second marriage began to fall apart, slowly but surely, because it had been based on too much sorrow and guilt, and not enough friendship or love. Rick agreed to let the boys stay with me after we separated, but then their father found out. He took them away from me on the Fourth of July weekend 1973, with barely enough time for us to say good-bye.

The night before they left for Saigon, Robbie came into my room, sat next to me on my bed and cried inconsolably. He said, "I know that if I go away, you will die, and I'll never see you again."

Our house was so empty after Derek and Robbie left. On the day before Thanksgiving, I got the news that, while the boys had been playing on a roof, Robbie fell into some high tension wires, was electrocuted and died. He was thirteen. Like so many boys who were victims of that war, he is buried somewhere in Saigon.

I blanked out a lot of what happened after that. My dad died, and my mom moved to the West Coast. I was planning to join her, needing someone to take care of me so badly. Then I met Ben, a divorced lawyer with five teenage daughters. Mom was so proud that I was dating an attorney.

Ben reassured my mom that he knew how hard my life had been and told her, "Trust me. She'll never have to worry about anything again."

I didn't know Ben very well when I married him, but I knew his daughters liked me. Ben thought I would be happier if we had a child together. A few months after we were married, I went to the doctor to see if it was safe to get pregnant. He informed me that I already was!

When Abby was born, I believed I had finally been forgiven. She was so wonderful! Then, a few months after her birth, I began to notice strange quirks in Ben's personality. I think he had married me to replace the "wife unit" in his life. He became verbally abusive and had ongoing scary outbursts that were directed at either one of his daughters or me. The daughters and I helped take care of whoever's turn it was to be "it," but after they all moved out, I was "it" all the time.

I stayed for seven years, thinking it was what I deserved. After all, I had been allowed to have Abby—how greedy could I be? What right did I have to want anything more? But as time went on, I started to see what was happening at home contrast more and more with the rest of my life.

Molly, a wonderful woman who was my boss at the State of Minnesota, encouraged me to try new things. I edited the newsletter and even applied for her job when she left. I became financial officer of the project and, with the support of some friends, identified my skills as a counselor. I was told that I had a knack for helping people identify their problems and bring out their own resources to deal with them. I became a volunteer at the local rape center. Within a year I was offered a full-time job!

As a victim advocate/crisis intervention worker and community educator, I was confident in my abilities. I loved what I was doing. I was amazed by all these incredible women who were finding strength to change their lives— sometimes with my help! Yet, ironically, there I was, still stuck in yet another abusive relationship.

As I became more and more worthy in my own eyes, it became clear that I needed to leave my marriage. I left Ben for my own happiness, and so that Abby could look forward to a better life than she saw her mother having.

By that time I was thirty-five years old and fifty pounds overweight. But it was the first time since I was a little girl that I was comfortable with myself again. I was able to be a nurturing mother to Abby, who thrived physically and emotionally.

In celebration of my new independence, I hung brightly colored pieces of paper on the mirrors and walls of our new apartment that read "NO LIES!" I worked hard at my job and made wonderful friendships with women and men. Being alone and without a primary relationship with a man was better than the other ways I had lived.

Since I was finally comfortable being alone, isn't it only natural that I would finally meet the right man for me? I had first been introduced to Abe years before when he had come to visit Marta, my boss from the Rape Center. They had been friends since college and met occasionally for lunch. Abe was a nice Jewish guy—nice looking, too. But I'm sure he never noticed me. I was just another woman at the office, fifty pounds overweight and married.

Later, when I ran into Abe at a work-related party, I had lost weight and gained confidence. I asked him to dance, and he refused, which was deflating, but Marta encouraged me to pursue him. She had talked to him about me, and she said he sounded interested.

"I think you should call him and ask him to meet you for a drink," she said in her firmest boss voice.

I gave Abe a call the following week, figuring I had nothing to lose. We met at a classy old hotel bar the night of the all-star game, 1982. I didn't realize it at the time, but Abe had made a great sacrifice to meet me that night. He's a baseball fanatic. He actually weeps at the last game of the world series because baseball is over for the season. He cries for happiness each spring at the beginning of the season, too. He did get home that night in time to catch the last few innings. As he pointed out, the all-star game doesn't really count anyway. Everybody always knows who's going to win.

Abe and I have been together since that night at the bar. I thought I'd never see him again after the night I told him I loved him. He also had been married before. It took a very long time for either of us to trust that our relationship would work.

We live in a big old house in St. Paul and work together to take care of it. Thirteen years now and our marriage is stronger than ever. Maybe it's because we were both married before and have learned from those experiences. Maybe it's because we don't need to *make* each other happy— or *make* each other anything. He refuses to make me respectable—he just respects me. And he loves me. Abby thinks of Abe as a third parent and loves him very much. She celebrates Father's Day with her father and "Abe's Day" with Abe a week later.

Almost immediately after Abe, Abby, and I moved in together, it was discovered that I had a large ovarian tumor. We were terrified that I had cancer.

Bette

The tumor was benign, but the scare started me thinking about my son again. Ovarian cancer is almost always fatal. What if he came looking for me, and I was dead?

Ever since the laws had changed in Minnesota, allowing children to attempt to find their birth parents, I had fantasized that one day my son would find me. I thought about it every day in the shower, which was almost the only time I was alone. But I had never thought about it the other way around until the cancer scare.

I wrote to the social service agency and asked them to find my son's family—to let them know that I, a stable woman (as stable as I'd ever been at least!) with a good marriage, a job, and a child of my own, would be open to contact with their son if they thought it was in his best interest. His family waited for a couple months to tell him. The day after he got the news he called the agency to set up our first meeting.

It was two weeks before Christmas, the year my son turned twenty. I drove to the agency by myself, was shown to a room and seated at a table to wait. I knew his name was Justin. I've never been so nervous. I had tried to prepare myself for every possible reaction he might have to me—from hatred to anger to blame to confusion as to why I had given him up. But I wasn't prepared for what really happened.

A beautiful young man entered the room. I stood, extended my hand to him and began to cry. Ignoring my outstretched hand, he put his arms around me and held me close. "It's all right now, it's all right," he said as he patted my back gently.

Imagine. My grown up child, comforting *me*, after all I had done! Then we talked. We talked about everybody and everything.

I was overwhelmed by the familiarity of him. We had so much in common. We drove the same make of car. We even had many of the same mannerisms—like pulling at the collars of our turtlenecks. His sense of humor and mine were just the same. Justin looked just like those old pictures of Dad that Mom had always kept. He looked almost exactly like my nephew. But it was more than just looks. He seemed like family. I felt like I had known him for a long, long time.

We talked about heredity and coincidence. My dad had been a jazz pianist and choir director, and my son played jazz piano and had been student director of his college choir. My dad had been an ambulance attendant in his youth and a volunteer police officer. My son had been an emergency medical technician and later became a volunteer police officer, too.

Like mine, Justin's life hadn't been easy. He had been to hell and back with chemical dependency and had a difficult relationship with his mother. When I showed him pictures of my father and my nephew, he said that was the first time he had seen anyone who looked like him, and that it made him feel less lonely.

He wanted me to meet his parents right away, but I was worried about doing further damage to his family life.

He made sure that I understood that he loved his folks, and then he said, "You're in my life now, and that's important to me. Our relationship has nothing to do with my folks, so don't worry about it."

Kind of unrealistic, but it made me feel better.

We all gathered at a restaurant for our first meeting, which was a bit of a fiasco. I liked Justin's girlfriend, Heidi, immediately, but his parents didn't approve of her because they were living together before marriage. There was so much tension at that table! It's hard for me to admit, but I felt resentment toward his folks. I was grateful to them for everything they had given him, but at the same time I resented them for it.

His dad, a Lutheran minister, was very kind and talked a lot about redemption that night. His mother tried to be kind, but I think she resented me for coming back into Justin's life. Instead of bringing photos of Justin at various ages, it seemed that all the photos were of her with him. I got the feeling that she didn't want me to forget who his real mother is. Of course I know that she is his mother. I know that all those years are lost to me, and that is one of the greatest griefs of my life.

When I first told Mom about meeting Justin, she told me that she always wanted me to keep him and never understood why I gave him up. I think we may have both rewritten history to comfort ourselves and will never know exactly what took place back then. Mom couldn't stop crying when she first met him. And she couldn't stop staring at him. He looked so much like Dad! I think it was hard on Mom when I said it was time for everybody to know about Justin, but she brags about him now.

Abby adores Justin and knew about my son ever since she was about six. That was when she asked me, "Mom, did you ever have any other children?" Of course I told her the truth.

Abe and Justin are still trying to figure out their relationship together, but they do have a mutual interest in music and enjoy each other's company.

I decided that the best way for me to be part of Justin's life was to let him initiate the contacts with me. That way, it was all on his terms according to his needs. But sometimes when I don't hear from him for a while, I violate my own rules and call him. We seem to need each other. When he's stressed or worried about something, he calls me to talk it over. When big things happen in his life, he wants to share them with me.

Abby, Abe, and I were at the wedding when he married Heidi. We were there with family and best friends on the terrifying night when their daughter Jessica was born prematurely at only twenty-three weeks, and again a week later when she had to have heart surgery.

Justin wanted us at the funeral when his father died, after a heartbreaking battle with brain cancer. He was very close to his adopted father, who was a strong and good man.

Justin's mother, a home economics teacher, has survived her own battle with cancer and a crippling car accident. Since her husband died, and despite all her problems, she has managed to finish her master's degree. She is a very strong-willed woman, and I've come to admire her. We have occasional phone conversations about our pride and worries regarding "our" son. Who knows— we might even end up being friends.

My job now is as an advocate for victims of crime in our county attorney's office. I help people deal with the effects

Bette and her son

of murder, rape, and violence of all sorts. It's exhausting but important work, and I'm good at it. Weekends, I'm often out in my perennial garden—it's good therapy for me. I also love entertaining and am a "dynamite cook," or so my friends say.

Mom lives with us, which presents a whole new set of joys and difficulties. She recently turned eighty and is still going strong. We have much to celebrate—we host a lot of celebrations at our house, including an annual after-Christmas holiday with Justin, Heidi, and Jessica, my miracle grandchild.

Justin, Heidi, and Jessica have moved back into his mother's house just outside of the Twin Cities. Because of her health problems, she was not able to maintain the home, so she had it remodeled into a duplex. They share it with her. I am proud of him for being a good son to her.

He is a wonderful son to me, too. I don't see him very often, but I know where he is, and he knows where I am. Heidi and I have a good relationship, and Jessica is a beautiful, bright, dark-eyed girl, full of life and full of herself—not unlike me as a child!

Abby has moved into her own apartment with two other young women and is attending technical school. She's an intelligent and lovely nineteen-year old, still a little unsure of her place in the world. I know in my heart that she will be happy and successful in all the ways that matter.

My stepdaughters, the five girls Abby's father had when I married him, still keep in contact with us. They all have happy lives now and bring their children to visit me every so often.

Derek, the brother of Robbie who died in Vietnam, has become a television personality, and I haven't heard from him for a while. I do sometimes speak to his uncle Rick (whom I believe to be Justin's father), so I know Derek is fine. For whatever reason, Rick does not want to meet Justin. There is nothing I can do about that, and Justin is dealing with it in his own way.

One day Justin and Heidi invited us to join them at Heidi's parents' country home. They took us on a fun, little tour of the town, and I felt so happy just being with them. In the newly remodeled town meeting hall, I found myself apart from the rest of the people and wandered into one of the rooms. Justin was seated there at the piano, his back to me. He was playing a song I remember my dad playing in

Bette

the church on Staten Island when I was a little girl. As I stood watching him, I felt as if a huge, precious part of my life had been given back to me—the good memories of my father—a gift from my son.

So life goes on. Justin's presence now is as permanent as I once thought giving him up was. For the first time, I can picture my future without dreaming of how things should be better. Being with Justin always brings a jumble of emotions. Joy because he wants me with him, pain about what has been lost, and uncertainty about what the future holds. I know I can't control anything, and I'm just trying to enjoy what is here for me now.

* * *

Chapter Six

❧ *Phoebe* ☙

In the 1940s and 1950s, when everyone seemed happy and normal, I felt defective. I grew up knowing I was different—shorter, thinner, darker and smarter than little girls were supposed to be. My looks might have been attributed to my Jewish heritage, but nobody ever explained that to me. In fact, my parents never talked about being Jewish, although I have no real evidence they tried to conceal it. At my school in Washington, D.C., all the popular girls had blonde ringlets and played kickball. I was always last to be picked for the team, and I couldn't blame them. I wasn't very good at it.

I tested positive for tuberculosis when I was five, which turned out to be some kind of family secret. One more thing that wasn't discussed. Somehow I got the idea that going to school might kill me. So I stayed home "sick" a good deal of the time. I would curl up in the window seat and daydream about being a famous cowgirl movie star, a mountain climber, or an astronaut. I never imagined myself as an ordinary flesh-and-blood woman—let alone a wife and mother.

Friends? Well, I didn't know how to talk to those girls at my school, but I managed to make about one friend a year. Everything would be okay for a while—until she would decide I was too weird and dump me.

Boys didn't like me either. I remember once, when I was in sixth grade, we were playing spin the bottle. When the bottle pointed to me, the boy screamed and ran away. Another time when I was older, my date left me to go necking with another girl.

Phoebe

I had a lot of confused feelings about sex and my body. My mother tried to teach me in a matter-of-fact way, but some of the "facts" were confusing. She took me to see an animated film about menstruation when I was in fifth grade, but I didn't understand it. My father seemed upset about sexuality issues. My notions of sex and shame were all mixed up together. Although sex wasn't treated as sinful, it was certainly dirty and embarrassing. I had to always be careful of bodily excretions, always be clean and never embarrass myself by needing to leave class to use the toilet. In fact, all bodily functions—from stomach rumbles to gas to eating heartily—were to be avoided.

My parents both worked for the federal government. Father was an attorney, and Mother held a secretarial job until I was born. My father loved me best; my mother loved my brother best and loved my father more than he loved her. She always seemed so sad. I blamed myself for adding to her sadness by staying home "sick" so often. I wrote in my diary, "I feel guilty about causing her unhappiness and aging." I think my mother's unhappiness and dissatisfaction made it hard for me to see myself as a normal wife and mother. My strongest memory about being a teenager is how angry my mother and I were with each other. It was a quiet, festering kind of anger rather than a yelling and screaming kind. Our family would never yell and scream.

In 1955, when I was sixteen, I began exploring Freud and motivational theories. It helped me get over my guilt, but it didn't help my relationship with my mother. In high school I found a group of people to whom academic success was attractive. For the first time in my life, I was popular! I finally had friends, and that helped my self-image tremendously.

My relative popularity continued at Cornell University in Ithaca, New York, where I got caught up in philosophical conversation and friendship with a group of other bright young math and physics majors. Most of them were males, and they were as naive about sex as I was. I must have dated sixty or so of these guys but we never progressed beyond necking. Besides, I was always afraid my stomach would rumble or I'd say something stupid. Still, I fell in love four times that first year at Cornell. And when it became clear that nobody loved me back, I became too sad to study and too depressed to go to class.

Phoebe, 1964

I went back to Washington a miserable failure. My parents treated me as if I were ill, and we all believed I was recovering from a nervous breakdown. After only a few months at my parents' house, I couldn't take it anymore. I moved to New York City in the spring and found my first lover, as a way to finally break free of my past. I enrolled in summer school at Columbia and afterwards took a trip out West with some acquaintances from school.

I enjoyed Yosemite and San Francisco, but I fell in love with Berkeley, where I decided to go for graduate study. When I returned to Cornell, it was as a witty and intellectually sophisticated philosophy major. I felt profoundly changed.

My ability to love normally was shaken again during my senior year at Cornell. When Chuck and I tried to have sex, he was unable to enter me. Chuck became very angry and accused me of having a "castrating vagina" and "unconscious anger." He told me I needed psychoanalysis, and I agreed. Even though I later learned of his ambivalence about women, I still thought there was something wrong with me—that maybe I was frigid. After all, my love experiences sure didn't read like the pages of D.H. Lawrence!

I moved to California for my graduate studies at University of California, Berkeley. There I met Paul, whose face was badly scarred from an accident. I admired his courage but felt uncomfortable about the stares he received when we were together. I started feeling guilty again, thinking about all my failures in intimate relationships. I dropped out of school, but I couldn't find a job. I said to myself, "I can't seem to have a long term relationship, so I must be weirder than I thought. I must be immature." I began therapy.

Phoebe

My therapist, a male who had little insight into women's issues, agreed that I was sick, and therapy continued. Nevertheless, I enrolled in college again and earned my master's degree in creative writing. Academics have always been the easiest part of my life. In 1965, when I was twenty-six, I met Randall, who had great empathy for all kinds of people—even weird ones like me. It seemed that his love was a natural love, and I thought I could learn to love naturally from him. But, like all the others, he left me. Feeling myself lacking once more, I seriously questioned my own ability to ever give or have a real or natural kind of love. Little did I know that we'd meet again.

The anti-war movement was my salvation. I was surrounded by a whole community of peace-loving, anti-war people. By working as a reporter for the Berkeley *Barb* and participating in demonstrations against the war in Vietnam, I was perfectly positioned to seek and learn the natural, all-giving love.

I was in the kitchen at the *Barb* when he arrived. Blonde, tall, blue-eyed and chain-smoking French cigarettes, Jim was a real man—100 percent pure macho. He was one of the more flamboyant anti-war organizers, and I was enchanted.

The first words he spoke to me were, "If you really want to end the war, why aren't you checking out the Redwood City thing?" I had been trying for weeks to discover details about a certain planned action in Redwood City—which was rumored to be more than just civil disobedience. We made a date for that Saturday to look at the napalm bomb storage sites.

The following week, I wrote a provocative article about him and the napalm escort truck he decorated with bright red fire extinguishers and a sign reading "Caution—Napalm Bombs Ahead." This was one of the biggest scoops I'd ever had. And probably the biggest crush—on a true hero of the movement. I tried very hard to be natural and open with him.

I became pregnant the first time we made love. Even though I was twenty-seven, I was naive about when in a woman's cycle she can conceive. I didn't realize that I had become pregnant. By the time I did figure it out, Jim had already left me.

Since I was still in therapy and this was Berkeley in the 1960s, I did have the option of a therapeutic abortion. I knew several doctors who would recommend it for me. The choice of abortion was still illegal in this country, and the therapeutic label was one of the ways people got around that. Most of the women I knew within the movement who got pregnant had abortions. But I wanted to do the loving thing, the giving thing. I contacted Jim to find out what he would want me to do. His response was, "I wish I could care, but I have no feelings about anything anymore."

To me, it was a matter of life and love. I would give the child to a good two-parent family. And besides, everybody knew this wasn't "the important stuff." What was important was to be a loving, natural person and to stop the war. One of my friends in the movement, Ted, promised to help me through the pregnancy.

This was August 1966, the beginning of the Port Chicago Vigil, an anti-war action targeting the Concord Naval Weapons Station, a major shipping point for arms to Vietnam. In Port Chicago, I saw firsthand people actually risking their lives out of genuine love for people they would never meet. We had to stop the shipment of arms! One night during a demonstration, Ted ran out in front of a truck that was moving too fast to stop. I was sure he would be killed—but I couldn't move. It was as if my feet were glued to the street. It was horrible, and I believed it was because of my inability to love that I couldn't help him. Luckily, someone else pushed him out of harm's way. At a later demonstration, when he stepped in front of a truck again, I did move— risking everything to help him. Then I realized that I did know how to love— that somewhere very deep I had always been able to love. It was a fragile knowledge, though, like the child growing inside me.

My friends in the movement treated my pregnancy as a temporary set-back, impatient for me to be my old self again. Due to my increasing size, I had to give up attending the demonstrations, but I followed all the anti-war activities closely and continued writing articles for the *Barb*.

Some of the Port Chicago people visited me from time to time to offer their support. I remember one guy who questioned my decision about adoption. "How can you give up your own child?" he asked incredulously. But I was only shocked that he could take the child's welfare so lightly as to suggest a course of action that would obviously not be good for the child.

Phoebe

I never told my parents that I was pregnant. They would have wanted me to come home, and I didn't want to be trapped—or have the child trapped either. I was afraid it might kill my father, who was so upset by sexual matters and loved me so much. No matter how they might have acted—urging me to keep or give up the child—they would have treated me as "ill" and "needing help" like when I flunked out of Cornell.

I never reconsidered my decision to give up the child. My therapist probably should have examined the options with me, but he didn't. No one in my intellectual radical peer group was raising a child alone. I never even considered it.

Radicals in Berkeley in 1967 did not go to homes for unwed mothers, but neither did we know much about adoption. I had an idea of wanting an open adoption, where I could meet the parents and approve of them, but for some reason I put off making any arrangements. I even put off finding an obstetrician until my seventh or eighth month. During this time, I felt anger and despair because Ted had also seemingly abandoned me. The joy of knowing I had always known how to love was now mixed with fear and sadness. But I never felt sad about giving up the child, because I closed that off for the child's sake.

In early February 1967, I met with a lawyer, but he refused to handle an adoption because I couldn't give him enough information about the father. So I signed up with an agency that I heard was the best around. My tenuous grip on my ability to love was still too new and untried when, a few days later, my son was born.

I had my first pains while working on a poster for the Port Chicago Vigil. I went to the clinic and told them I was in labor. After checking me, they told me to go home and come back when the pains were five minutes apart. I remember Ted and his new girlfriend Patrice, along with other Port Chicago people, took care of me that day as if we were family. They drove me to the hospital when the time came, but then I was alone.

In the labor room, I told one of the nurses that I was scared. She said, "You knew what you were getting into when you did it." Ted came for a quick visit and said he'd return, but he never did. I spent a lot of my labor time going back and forth in my mind between loving him and hating him, all the time trying to be loving and giving. At some point, I realized I needed to focus on the birth and try to relax. I had no childbirth training but seemed to know this instinctively.

There was one long pain, and I felt triumph and joy as the baby came out. He was beautiful, four pounds twelve ounces and eighteen inches long. I wanted to hold him right away, but they had to take him to the nursery because he was so small. He was kept in an isolette, and I only held him two or three times. One of those times, I felt a strong need to unwrap the blanket and look at his toes. They were long and thin like mine, and such tenderness built up inside me. But then he started to cry, and I thought I was hurting him or doing something wrong, so I had him taken back to his isolette.

I cried constantly and didn't know why. The head nurse was from India, and she talked to me very gently and kindly. "I've seen many people give up their babies. Some show nothing; some cry. Do you want to talk about it?" I told her about my decision and about my faith in other parents to raise this child. I didn't tell her that I resented the shot that they gave me to dry up my milk and my emotions.

After I signed the papers allowing the agency to take the baby from the hospital when he was ready, I stood at the nursery window to see him one final time. He looked so small in that big room. In my mind I named him Nathan Steven Goldman, after my deceased grandfather, aware that this was a strangely Jewish thing for me to do.

Everybody reassured me that he'd be out of the isolette soon and go briefly to a foster home before being adopted. I left the hospital alone.

One of the Port Chicago people offered to let me stay at her apartment until I recovered. In my continuing efforts to love freely, I studied her relationships with her friends and even patched up a fight between Ted and his girlfriend Patrice. The night after I helped them, I remember wondering why I was feeling so suicidal. That afternoon I had gone to the adoption agency, held my three-week-old son for the last time and signed the adoption papers. I couldn't understand why everyone was being so over-emotional. There were tears in the social worker's eyes.

I spent the next few weeks resting and weaving little God's eyes out of toothpicks and embroidery thread. Each brightly-colored layer of thread wove a mandala of love—of reaching forth and giving—rather like knitting baby booties. In April I took part in the mobilization against the war in Vietnam, continuing my quest to love through activism.

Phoebe

In May, when the child was almost four months old, the agency called to say he had been placed with a family. I was upset. "What took so long? I thought he would be with a family right away."

The social worker replied, "But he was so small, dear, and you put so many restrictions. . . ." I was surprised that they had actually paid attention to my requests—that he not be placed with a military, police or strictly religious family. Though I didn't like the idea of him spending so much time in foster care, the description of his family sounded good. They "hold hands and touch a lot, are sensitive and educated, and they love him very much." One parent was Jewish and one was not. Just like his real parents.

I told my mother about the child shortly thereafter, when she phoned to tell me about my father's serious heart attack. I told her to tell him, if there was a need. She said, "If the child's not with you, how can it help?" My father died shortly thereafter, never knowing he had a grandson.

For the next two years, I lived "as if." I called it that. I lived as if by reaching out, as if with love, I would find someone reaching too, whose love would call to mine. Living "as if" saved me from despair and gave me the energy to do things—to attend demonstrations, force myself into relationships and develop a collective radical magazine. I also formed a women's group, though I was certainly not one of those people needing "women's liberation."

The people I knew recognized that I had passed through a great change. "You're one of the sanest persons I've ever known," was what one woman told me. It was not exactly false, but it left out all the despair and loss I was trying to ignore.

Eventually I went full circle, returning to Randall, whom I'd loved in 1965. I fell in love with him all over again, denying the fact that he would never love me as much as I loved him. I seemed to be playing out some role—clinging to him and even following him to Europe for three years.

My mother came to visit me in France. Sitting across from each other at a sidewalk cafe, I remember the sweet smell of flowers from the street vendors. We talked about my father's death, about my giving birth, about being mothers. It was the last time I saw her alive. It was in that cold Paris winter that I received the news of my mother's death. I finally let myself despair. I wrote in my journal, "Every loss is the loss."

I moved back to Berkeley at age thirty-five. Nathan would have been seven then. From when he was very little I always promised myself, "When my son is ten, I'll go ask the agency about him." By then, I figured he'd be so much a part of his adoptive family that it couldn't hurt. The social worker who met with me had a warm smile and a caring heart. She gave me a photograph of Nathan taken when he was two weeks old. There were tears in her eyes, but I didn't cry.

On the way home, I wrote in my notebook every detail of information she had given me. The parents were about my age, open and sensitive. One was a professor, one a medical technician. They loved their child who at ten months was already talking, weighed twenty-one pounds and walked holding onto the furniture. He had black wiry hair. My hair! That was all. The agency had no further contact after the adoption was finalized. I was grateful for the good information and tried not to be sad that there was nothing more recent.

The next month, I found out I was pregnant again. The father was Jake, who I'd been seeing for three years. He was divorced and estranged from his three daughters. Jake wanted me to have an abortion, and I agreed at first, even making the appointment at the clinic. But I couldn't go through with it.

When I called Jake in tears to tell him, he said, "Then I will never see you again. This child should not be born." He believed that any child of his would be doomed.

So there I was, alone again. But this time things would be different. This time I would do everything right. I would get the best medical care and find the best adoptive parents. Though I knew there would probably be no more babies for me, I planned to give up this child too.

Through mutual friends I found a wonderful, sympathetic couple who were unable to have children of their own. They were delighted with the prospect of raising my child. Over the next months, we developed a close trusting relationship, even deciding together on a pediatrician. But in the end, I couldn't do it. I couldn't give up another child. I gave birth to my second son, whom I named Jerald.

I was convinced that God wanted me to keep this baby, and at the same time God seemed to be saying to me, "If they keep him he'll die. If you keep him he'll only go mad from your insanity."

88

Phoebe

I was so confused. I contacted the couple who wanted Jerald. They were willing to take him even though I warned them, "I have not decided yet. I may take him back." From the time he was four weeks old until he was four months old, Jerald was with that couple. It was so hard for me to hurt them, I almost didn't take him back. But I realized that I could raise him—I could raise my own child. I offered to let them visit him and they did, but after a few weeks they said it hurt too much, and they stopped coming. Nobody else came to see us either. I was alone with the baby and the landlady and neighbors, who complained about his crying at night. We moved when Jerald was a year old; he still cried at night, and a whole new set of people began complaining. I was getting desperate and even yelled at him and spanked him to try to get him to stop crying. I was afraid we'd end up homeless, afraid I'd have to give him up—all the while thinking that maybe I should give him up.

I couldn't completely accept the fact that I had the right to be his mother and he my son. I could not go on building a life around this family unit nor raise him properly as my son. At the same time, I was terrified of losing Jerald. This is how my second son became a victim of circumstance—a victim of my relinquishing his older brother.

On January 19, 1991, I returned home from work after picking up my thirteen-year old, emotionally troubled, second son from therapy. Reaching into the mailbox, I saw the adoption agency's return address. Six years earlier I had sent a letter to the agency, enclosing a picture of myself in case Nathan should ever inquire about me. I had never received a response. Inside the envelope was a legal form, a "Waiver of Confidentiality" form, which I signed, had notarized and mailed the next day.

Two weeks later, when Nathan had just turned twenty-four, I couldn't wait any longer and called the agency from my office. The social worker said, "Your son came in to ask about you. He was very concerned that you should know he has a good life." They had given him my letter and picture and had said, "He was very moved." She described him as a sensitive and intelligent artist and designer. I was sitting in my drab office, trying to grasp that this was really happening. My son was real—a sensitive young man. An artist. My son!

He sent the agency a letter and some photos for me. The photos were all in color, and it was as if color had just entered the world. His eyes were like mine, his hands, the line of his jaw, his ears—and this letter, his touch, with thoughts he had written—this time I had to try very hard not to cry. He said he was going to Europe for a month and could we meet when he returned?

On April 8, I got a phone call from the agency. My son was back from his trip and wanted to meet at the agency. "He's a little frightened about meeting you," the worker said. I left work early on Friday, April 12, to meet the son I had given up twenty-four years before. "Charles is here waiting for you. He's very nervous."

All I could think of was to hurry so he wouldn't be nervous anymore. "It's important to have no expectations," the social worker told me.

A young man in a striped shirt was standing up. His hair was lighter than I thought it would be, and he seemed so young, so serious. I opened my arms and cried, "You're my kid!" He was crying as we moved together, holding each other. His arms were around my neck, I touched his hair. This was real. We held each other for a long time, crying and talking. We exchanged phone numbers—he lived in Berkeley—and our hearts touched.

Those first weeks, we spent a lot of time absorbing the reality of each other. My senses were full of him. Over and over again, we said things like "I know" and "It's all right now" and "You didn't know, you couldn't know." We were helpless in that time of bonding, in celebration, and adoration. We are so much alike. Our faces and bone structures, tastes and politics, prayers and hopes—all the same. We even finish sentences for each other.

In time, we lightened up some. I told him about the reasons for my relinquishing him, and he told me about the hole he had inside him, in spite of having a loving family. He confided in me about the close call with the other self he might have been, if I had raised him.

Jerald was very enthusiastic about the reunion and couldn't wait to meet Charles. But Charles and I kept putting off the meeting of these half brothers because it might be too intense and confusing for Jerald. They did eventually meet a few times, but maybe because of the age difference, never really hit it off.

Phoebe

My needs began to drive our relationship. More and more often, I became the one who asked to meet. I knew I should limit myself but I couldn't. Jerald needed so much of my time, and Charles seemed to need less and less of it.

I'm afraid I pushed too much because in July he started shortening our meetings. By August he was often "busy," and by September he was distant when we met, although he reassured me that nothing was wrong. When I insisted on an explanation, he finally admitted that he was having trouble balancing the intensity of our new relationship with his love for his parents. "They are my parents," he said, "however it happened. I'm who I am now. You are a stranger—I don't really mean that—but I'm not in the same place as when we first met."

Charles told me that his adoptive parents had encouraged him to find me, but they did not wish to be part of his relationship with me, see pictures of me or know anything about me. I don't know how much their response to our reunion affected him. Charles moved down the coast to continue his art studies. We only see each other once or twice a year but talk regularly on the phone.

Phoebe, 1993

I feel as if we have a good relationship growing. I have a sense of freedom that we can talk when we have something to tell each other. Sometimes our conversations are full of laughter and ease, and sometimes there is a tension, as if our thoughts are too close, too identical. Sometimes I fear I have lost him again, but I know this bond cannot be lost. My son is real, a wonderful, caring person. And usually he sounds glad to hear my voice.

Life has opened up for me since I met Charles. I am more able to enjoy the pleasures of life—like driving to the mountains or watching a movie. Over the years, I've developed an understanding of my own ways of dealing with my feelings about closure and love. I think I can now identify what is real and valuable.

My relationship with my second son has changed since my reunion with my first son. Jerald is doing well in his special high school and will graduate next year. He was in his early teens when Charles found me; I was so focused on Charles during those first months, I was not able to give much attention to Jerald's emotional needs. I feel a stronger connection to Jerald now and try to play a supportive role in his therapy.

I feel sad that my sons are not close. Jerald hoped for a strong relationship with his newfound brother, but Charles has avoided getting close to him. Maybe he sees in Jerald the kinds of problems he might have had, if he had spent his life with me. Or maybe their personalities are too different.

I had hoped that my two sons would be more like a family, though I never expected to compete with his adoptive family. Charles says that his family is not at all disturbed by his finding me—that they are secure with their son. I think that security is partially because I am so unreal to them. I would like to know them, but I can live with their distance if it does not affect my relationship with Charles.

Mostly I am joyous and glad that my son found me. We get along well except when I see his avoidance of me as avoidance of things with which he has not dealt. But I no longer dwell on the negatives, and I want to believe that I will never again get lost in my insecurities. I am working to develop strong mother/son relationships. With both my sons. After all, the bond of love is there, has always been there, and will remain.

* * *

Chapter Seven

֍ *Shirley* ֎

My sister, Marilyn ("Muff"), and I grew up in what we grimly called "The Sanatorium." It was a rather dreary existence for both of us and an unusual way for children to be raised, to put it mildly. I was born in Boston in 1929, six months before my father was diagnosed with tuberculosis. By the time I was four, it became clear that he would never recover, and my mother thought it best to move to Pennsylvania where his family lived.

I remember our new ten-room house was big and airy, with a giant elm tree in the front. This old elm was the largest tree in the area, and it became very special to me. For years, when I was upset about things, I would sit at its base and just let my thoughts go. My tree was also the first in the area to contract the dreaded Dutch elm disease. I was so upset when they cut it down.

Mother began transforming rooms, one by one, into sickrooms as terminally ill relatives moved in with us. Arthritic and elderly Great Aunt Maggie was first, and of course there was my father. As his disease worsened, he was admitted to hospitals and sent home repeatedly. Poor Father. I never knew him as a father— only as a patient. He and I really had no relationship. I was only twelve when he died. My sister was six when he died, so neither of us ever really had a father.

After Father died, it was somehow determined that Mother was the only one in our extended family able-bodied enough to handle sick people. And heaven knows, we had the space. Society was different in the 1930s and 1940s. Family members relied more on each other than they do now. When people had trouble, they went to their families expecting to be taken in.

Next to arrive were the grandparents. Grandmother and Grandfather Munson came as a set. I believe they had heart trouble, as did Grandmother and Grandfather Holbrook, whose stays overlapped with the other grandparents' stays. My mother's sisters, Aunt Liza and Aunt Lorraine, both had cancer, as I recall. Father's brother Daniel and his wife, Elaine, had severe health problems due to excessive drinking. With the exception of Aunt Maggie, who spent the last few weeks of her life in a nursing home, all of these people died in our house.

The atmosphere was often hushed and gloomy. I can still hear my mother's voice reminding us, "Never talk in a loud voice" and "Don't run in the house" and "Don't walk with a heavy step." Mother was a good soul, and we were quite close. She always tried to make time for me between Aunt Maggie's feeding and Aunt Lorraine's sponge bath—or whenever she could spare a few minutes. Sometimes I'd follow her around, and we'd chat while she changed bedclothes, refilled water bottles and performed other seemingly endless chores.

Muff and I were not particularly close, partly because of the age difference. We were also treated very differently. With her delicate bone structure and soft blonde curls, Muff was the protected, dainty daughter. There were always grandparents, aunts and uncles, all in various stages of decay and decline, who had the time and inclination to teach "Little Muffie" the refined niceties of life. Muff learned cooking, sewing, needlework, piano, and fine manners.

As the older child in a fatherless family, I was treated as the man of the family and was expected to handle the heavy work around the house. I was groundskeeper and handyman, always working alone, my mind stagnant from lack of contact with other people. At the tender age of nine, I was already changing storms and screens, hauling them to and from the garage, up the rungs of the ladder and hanging them in the appropriate windows. I also mowed the lawn and painted the house—indoors and out. Consequently I became a tomboy, and though I was mostly a solemn and solitary child, I did have a few boys as pals.

There were several unspoken rules in our household. We were never to argue with anyone or criticize anyone or anything. Nor were we to show any emotion whatsoever. It was a puritanical environment. Conversations or even idle comments regarding dressing, undressing, getting ready for bed, or any act performed in the bathroom were all strictly forbidden. We were not allowed to talk about the body at all, so of course talking about sex was taboo.

94

Shirley

Since I was taught nothing about my body and nothing about sexuality, I was left to conjure up my own images and beliefs. I'm not sure where I got my ideas, but I believed that people's sexuality existed only in the sanctity of the marital bed. I believed that only in the union of marriage could a child be conceived. Of course, it would be a sin to enjoy sex, except in the sacrosanct domain of husband and wife.

I had little or no social life in grade school. I wasn't allowed to invite my few friends to my house, and I wouldn't have wanted to do so. Nobody would have had very much fun in that funereal environment. I pretended that I lived in a normal household and made up excuses if anyone wanted to come over. In those days, it was not appropriate for a girl to be as masculine as the role I was forced to play, so I hid that part of my life too. I developed strong coping skills, which helped me—for a time.

My teachers were impressed with how quickly I learned. I was always at the top of my class and was even able to skip second grade. The only other thing I remember clearly about those early school years was that, by the time I was in fifth grade, my grades gradually became deplorable. I believe it was because my depressing surroundings had caught up with me and affected my schoolwork. Because of the negative atmosphere, it was almost impossible for me to study at home. Things got so bad that I had to repeat fifth grade.

The United States entered World War II in 1941. I remember being at a restaurant and hearing the news about the bombing of Pearl Harbor. Subsequently, our class sold war bonds, but I don't think the war affected me greatly. I had to ride my bicycle to school because gasoline ration coupons were to be used sparingly. And I remember all of us sixth graders being bussed to a hilltop where we were supposed to help level the ground for an army airstrip. Of course I was well suited for that task!

Because my social skills were so stunted, I was very much a loner by the time I started junior high school. I worked hard and gradually started getting better grades. My social life improved along with my self-esteem. Although I didn't have an inkling as to what normal sexual maturing was like, I developed a few childlike crushes. I didn't know how to relate to boys in a romantic way and couldn't really understand the attraction of dating. I had friends who happened to be boys but no boyfriends until well into my college years.

High school began on a positive note. Although I still performed all the male-oriented tasks at home, I was starting to feel better about myself. I enjoyed learning, stimulating conversation, and sports. It's hard to say how things might have turned out because, when I was a junior, I had a terrible accident. During a diving lesson, I threw my legs up too far, causing a severe sprain in my back. The doctors said I was already unconscious when I hit the water. Due to the injury, I was forced to spend the next year in bed.

Strangely enough, I loved being the patient for a change. For the first time in my life, I was allowed to be weak—to need care and attention. Even though I was sorry to burden my mother with yet another person to care for, I felt like a queen bee. Luckily, it was around this time that my father's life insurance finally paid off, making it possible for Mother to hire a maid, laundress, and handyman.

After recovering from the acute stage of my back sprain, I wanted to get my high school diploma and make up for lost time. I completed the second half of my junior year and my senior year all in nine weeks!

College was a real eye-opener for me—socially, emotionally and sexually. I discovered that I was able to get along well with both girls and boys. I found I could carry on highly intelligent conversations and that people actually seemed to like me. Other girls started telling me that I was attractive, and boys started seeking me out. My puritanical tendencies were still very strong, but for the first time I was beginning to question them. I wanted to be popular and world-wise like the other girls. Most of all, I wanted to be well educated so that I could control my own destiny.

Once during the holidays, I brought home a girl I knew from school. My college friends were a very diverse and progressive group. We were an anti-sorority sorority—a bit of a clique opposed to cliques. My friend was black, and it never occurred to me that she wouldn't be welcome in our home. But when my mother came to the door she said, "You are welcome home, but *that* will never set foot in this house."

I couldn't believe it! Later, I found out that in addition to being racist, my mother was also anti-Semitic and anti-foreign-born. Topics such as politics, race relations, or foreign affairs had simply never been discussed in our home. I felt terribly disappointed in Mother. My friend and I turned on our heels and left. Mother and I never really resolved that issue between us. I knew she would never change, and she never did.

Maybe some talents run in the family, but I decided to become a nurse. I excelled at my college studies and maintained a 4.0 grade-point average. With my minor in psychology/sociology, I felt confident that I had found my niche. I was on top of the world.

In 1949, I met the only man in my life who could be both friend and lover to me. It was at a college party. His name was Russell, and we were a perfect match. With his craggy good looks, artistic prowess, and extreme intelligence, Russell was the only fellow that made any sense to me whatsoever. He was an "egghead" and liked classical music. We had so much in common. I remember at that first meeting I sat in a chair and Russell sat on the arm of the chair. Totally absorbed in each other, we discussed the deepest of subjects, oblivious to the beer-drinking madness around us.

Russell and I had a fantastic relationship and enjoyed everything together—music, theater, art, philosophy, religion, hiking, roller skating, dinners out, and quiet evenings at his apartment. Through him I learned a lot more about feeling confident about myself as a woman, self-expression, and, yes, sexuality.

I was terribly naive about sex and conception, and still maintained my belief that one had to be married and in a state of "holy bliss" in order to conceive a child. It seems unbelievable to me now that I was so badly informed. I was an intelligent young woman, writing articles for a psychology magazine, with an IQ way above average, with this incredible naiveté.

My "belief" was not challenged for more than a year, and Russell and I enjoyed a fulfilling sexual relationship. On New Year's Eve 1951, I became pregnant. At first I was elated, thinking that I had achieved that state of "holy bliss." Only, it wasn't exactly holy because I wasn't married. And Russell wasn't about to marry me. He was already married to a woman who lived out of town. I had known about Russell's marriage almost since the beginning of our relationship. Maybe I was lying to myself, but his being married never really bothered me—I figured it was his problem.

The thought of telling my mother about being pregnant was horrifying to me. I was afraid of what she might think and do, and I knew it would add to her burdens. I procrastinated as long as possible, and then told her. As I had feared, she was devastated. She insisted I remove myself to a home for unwed mothers in a nearby large city. In 1952, it was not proper for a girl of my class to have an illegitimate baby!

Russell was as adamant as Mother about my giving up the baby. He didn't want any of the complications, commitment, or responsibility. Russell was the only person other than Mother who knew about my pregnancy. The neighbors were told that I had gone off to a private school.

I finished the 1951-1952 college year and immediately moved to a home for unwed mothers. I liked it there. I worked in the office and found the work quite pleasant. Quite easy, in fact. Russell offered to pay my room and board and medical fees, which was decent of him. But when the baby was born, Russell crossed me off his list. I guess he thought he had done his part. He never wanted anything to do with me after that.

Shirley

Russell was the only man I ever really loved. In my mind, we were the perfect couple. The fact that we would never be married or even together again had nothing to do with my deep love for him. I know I will carry that love to my grave.

On October 2, 1952, I gave birth to a beautiful little boy whom I named Richard Holbrook Munson. I was allowed to stay with him at the home for one month, and then I was required to hand his tidy little body over to the adoption agency. It was a horrible feeling, letting go of my baby.

I returned home terribly depressed. Russell was becoming more and more distant and had no understanding about my feelings of love and loss for our son. Russell was—and is—extremely self-centered. I was disappointed that Russell couldn't understand my pain, but I worked hard at trying to forget about it.

Shirley

Three months later, before the finalizing of my son's adoption, the agency informed me that I could see him one last time. I was overjoyed. I went to the adoption agency and held Ricky in my arms. He was such a special little person! But I knew I was not to be part of his life. I gave him back to the social worker and went home.

Although I was suffering greatly, I began to pick up the pieces and resume my life. The local hospital hired me as an operating room technician due to my excellent grades and high recommendation from the college. I was the first OR technician in Pennsylvania, and I held that position for three years. Then I met the man who was to become my husband.

Bill was vibrant and fun when I first met him. I was twenty-six, he was twenty-eight—and single. I married him because I thought we had a lot in common. Like me, he enjoyed skiing, camping, and hiking, but he wasn't on a par with me intellectually. Ironically, it turned out that Bill experienced a puritanical upbringing, too. My husband was a very strange man. Conservative and unimaginative, Bill was a "square" and a "workaholic." Though we often disagreed, he never touched me in anger. In fact, he barely touched me much at all. Bill was practically asexual.

Within a year of our marriage, Bill was diagnosed with pernicious anemia, lupus, and diabetes—the same kinds of chronic illnesses that characterized my early life. Isn't it curious how the past revisits us?

Somehow, though, I managed to become pregnant four times. The first two pregnancies ended in miscarriage, which was incredibly sad for me. Then in 1961, I gave birth to a boy—another Ricky. A little more than one year later, I had Brenda.

When the children were ages four and five, it became evident that I was going to have to contribute to the family's income. I applied for a job as a kindergarten teacher. Teachers were scarce then, so I was hired, even though I had no formal teaching training. I was required, however, to complete my bachelor's degree. At the same time, I worked on my master's degree, which I earned summa cum laude.

I loved teaching and felt again like I had come into my own. I was able to combine much of what I'd learned in life with what I'd been taught in school. I felt like I was making an important contribution to society.

Though my marriage was dissatisfying, life was tolerable on the home front. Because of Bill's illnesses, I was in charge of the family. My earlier training as "man of the house" was good preparation, and this time I really enjoyed it—being my own boss in my own home.

I had a secret life, though. I still secretly grieved for my lost son. Every year on his birthday, I would burn a candle and play Ravel's *Pavane for a Lost Child,* a poignantly beautiful piece of classical music. More than a few tears were shed over the years. I worried about my lost son, thought occasionally about looking for him, but I had no idea where to begin. My other secret, of course, was that Russell was still the great love of my life.

The 1960s and 1970s passed by, and my children were growing up. As I recall, Bill was always either working at the office or sick in bed. His day job was that of a hydraulic engineer. Since that wasn't enough work for him, he also worked evenings for another company as a draftsman. The children didn't see much of him. Like me, they didn't have much in the way of a father figure. We all managed, though. I haven't been particularly close with either of my children, maybe because they've both inherited their father's nose-to-the-grindstone tendencies.

It seems that everything happened in 1980. My son Rick was involved in an automobile accident and was almost killed when his car broke in half around a telephone pole. Actually he "died" six times, but they "brought him back." He was teaching a friend to drive at the time, and nobody knows exactly what happened. The friend survived with only minor injuries but Rick ended up with two fractured arms, a broken back, a bruised heart, and heaven knows what else. He eventually recovered but has never seemed the same since. His attitude has turned negative and sour, which isn't conducive to friendship with others or his own happiness.

In December of 1980, several months after Rick's accident, I was alone in the house when the phone rang. A male voice said, "Shirley? Did your name used to be Shirley Munson?"

"Yes."

"This is Scott Richards."

I had no idea who Scott Richards was, so I said again, "Yes?"

Shirley

"Tell me, Shirley—what were you doing on the evening of October 2, 1952, at about 6:35 P.M.?"

I could barely speak. "I was having a baby," I finally croaked out.

"Ah! Well, I've changed a lot since you last saw me, Mom. I'm much taller now, and I have a beard."

I tried to picture him, my lost son, tall and with a beard. It suddenly occurred to me how much his voice sounded like Russell's. There were so many emotions jumbled up inside me, it took me awhile to respond. I couldn't get the words out. After what seemed like an hour, I said, "Hi, honey. I missed you."

Then the words poured out of both of us. I told him everything. I told him about when he was conceived, and my feelings for his biological father. I held nothing back from him.

Needless to say, I was thrilled. His last name was almost identical to the first name I had given him. We agreed that it was quite a coincidence and had a long and delightful conversation. I guess you could say we were attempting to catch up on the past twenty-eight years.

There was an instant closeness between us. He told me about his career as a computer consultant. It was a fascinating and high-paying position. He was in the process of writing a book having to do with two of his many passions—travel and computers.

Scott explained that in order to find me, he had first used some notes that were made by his adoptive mother around the time of the adoption. It had taken him a total of three months of casual research, guesswork, and cross-correlation to complete the search. After studying telephone directories and making many phone calls, he finally came up with his birth certificate from the state of Pennsylvania. He gave me his adoptive parents' phone number and suggested I give them a call. Then he wanted to know the name of his birth father.

I gave him Russell's name and told him that, the last I had heard, Russell was a jeweler in a town in upstate New York. Later, I found that within minutes of hanging up with me, he was talking to his biological father. This is how that conversation went:

"Hi, Russell. This is Scott Richards. Tell me—what were you doing on New Year's Eve 1951?" Scott just couldn't resist that one.

He discovered that Russell had five other children through five marriages. Like Scott, Russell held art and expression in the highest esteem. Writing and traveling also ran in the family. They made plans to meet.

Meanwhile, I called my mother to tell her about Scott's call. By this time Mother had buried all the terminally ill relatives and had moved to Florida to help my sister, Muff, take care of her children. Ever the caretaker, Mother. Although we had never discussed my baby, Mother's reaction to my son's surprise "appearance" was positive.

Muff had always known about my giving up my baby, though we had never discussed it, either. She was very happy for me. Muff and I had developed a good friendship, once we were away from "The Sanatorium." She had built a wonderful life for herself, getting her Ph.D. and becoming an administrator for the Florida public schools.

After that phone conversation, I called Scott's adoptive parents in Ohio and introduced myself. They were both extremely gracious and expressed a desire to meet me. I let them know that I was interested in meeting them, too.

Scott and I exchanged phone calls for the next few weeks. He flew to upstate New York to meet Russell and his half siblings. Scott eventually developed strong friendships with these people and now is in regular contact with them. After being raised an only child, Scott suddenly had scores of new relatives! He told me that the first time he met these people, he was amazed because everyone looked like him! Naturally, that had never happened before.

Russell thought it was great to have a ready-made son who appeared at age twenty-eight. No diapers, no adolescent crisis, no requests for money. Scott felt like he was a "chip off the old block" and had inherited Russell's distaste for commitment as well as his characteristic nose and lanky frame.

A few weeks after his meeting with Russell, Scott invited me to visit him in Ohio for five days. Our first meeting was ecstatic. We hugged tightly and then spent the whole afternoon getting to know each other and sharing photo albums. I knew we were soul mates. It was uncanny how much Scott looked and acted like Russell.

Shirley

That evening when darkness fell, Scott decided to entertain me with his highly technical "laser show" complete with music and special effects. He settled me into a comfortable chair and began preparing the projector and sound system. He told me that the choice of music was critical to the artistic integrity of the show.

The walls and ceiling of Scott's living room came alive with the magic of light. And then, imagine my amazement when the strains of *Pavane for a Lost Child* came to my ears! Although I fought for control over my emotions, I'm afraid I broke down a little. Scott put his arm around me gently.

"Shirley? Do you want me to turn on the lights? Shall I change the music? Are you okay?"

I turned to him and shook my head. "I'm fine. I just wonder how you came to choose this piece of music, that's all."

He said, "I don't know. It's been going through my head all day. I can change it. . . ."

Then I told him, "I have played this music every year on your birthday for twenty-eight years, while burning a candle in your memory."

Scott later confided that at that exact moment he actually felt our biological connection.

I also met Pauline and Earl, Scott's adoptive parents, during that first Ohio visit. Wealthy and well-educated, his parents were fine people, willing and able to give Scott many advantages I may not have been able to give him. Over the years, Pauline and I became quite close, exchanging letters and phone calls about our thoughts and experiences. Our lives seemed to have progressed in many similar directions.

Earl and I got along well, too. Years later, after both Pauline and Bill had passed away, we still maintained our friendship with letters and telephone calls. Earl recently wanted me to come to Ohio for a visit, but I declined. I am simply not the country club type. Not me. Earl has come out from under the shadow of his wife, who was dominant in their marriage. He is enjoying his life and lady friends.

Bill, Ricky, and Brenda were all happy that I was reunited with my son. Rick and Brenda, both in their twenties at the time, were reasonably excited about having a "new brother." As it ended up, Scott got along better with

Shirley and her birth son

Brenda than Rick, but that is possibly due to the personality changes from Rick's accident. Scott rarely sees my children, and I don't imagine he'll ever develop very much closeness with them. Too many differences, maybe.

Rick and Brenda have finished college, married and have children of their own. They are very conservative people—their father's children. They still think Scott is a little odd, and they probably think I am, too.

Scott and I continued our relationship, primarily with phone calls and letters. In 1982, he came to my home for Thanksgiving. My sister and her children from Florida joined us. We had a delightful family reunion, and Scott keeps in touch with his aunt and cousins to this day.

My workaholic husband Bill always said his life would be over when he retired at sixty-five, and he was true to his word. He retired from the engineering company, turned sixty-five in May and died in August.

Shirley

I, on the other hand, have found a certain freedom in retirement and growing older. After teaching for twenty years, I had to retire in 1984 when I had a small stroke. It wasn't serious, thank heavens, but it was just enough to keep me from teaching.

There was plenty to keep me busy, though. When Ricky and his wife were having marital problems, I took their children to live with me for a year, until their parents could begin getting along better. The children were safe and happy with me, and it was nice having young ones around again.

The past revisited again when my mother, aged and ill, came to live in my home for eighteen months. I was nursing my sick husband at the time, too. Knowing the end was near, Mother requested to be put in a nursing home, where she died, quietly and uncomplaining. She didn't want to burden me the way she had been burdened, dear soul.

In 1991, I started a little craft business with a friend. It started as a small time hobby, but has grown to be quite the cottage industry! We make crocheted towels, jackets, and other things and sell them at craft shows and malls in the area. I'm enjoying myself. The handwork keeps me busy, and the craft shows gets me out among people.

I have no regrets about my life and can now look back with happiness and fond memories. I feel immensely proud that Scott, with all his wisdom and intelligence, had the means to cut through the red tape and find me.

Since meeting and knowing Scott, I feel completely fulfilled—a feeling that even eclipses the disappointments of my marriage with Bill. It's as though the good things in my life have been enhanced by knowing him, while the negatives have been suppressed. I owe Scott my gratitude for making my life whole again. I thrill in knowing that he is alive and seeing him make a successful life for himself.

I am extremely happy that my continuing love for Russell materialized in our son in such a magical way. As I mentioned before, Russell has always been the only man I've ever loved. Even though Russell wants nothing to do with me, he can't take my love or the son born of that love, away from me.

The reunion with my son has somehow relieved me of a tremendous inner sorrow. All the years of being told what to do and what to think—coupled with my inability to meet all the unreasonable expectations—left scars on me. My early training and upbringing shattered my self-confidence. No matter how I fought to regain it, lasting self-confidence always eluded me.

Thanks to Scott's finding me, I've been able to view the past with a saner, more mature perspective. I can finally give myself credit for all that I've done and all that I've become. I have given the earth three very intelligent children, and I earned a master's degree cum laude. I am important in my own right—and a free spirit again, after all these years!

* * *

Chapter Eight

Julie

I grew up in a sleepy little town in northeastern Vermont, not far from the Canadian border. Born in 1951, I was the eldest of three. My sister, Stephanie, was two years younger than I, and our brother, Joseph, was four years younger than she. We lived in a small, rented house in a quaint little neighborhood, within walking distance of almost everything. I had many friends all up and down our street.

It was unusual for mothers to work during the 1950s, but mine did. Mom was a registered nurse in the operating room of a nearby hospital. She was admired by doctors and nurses alike because of her soft-spoken, yet authoritative, manner.

My dad worked in the car business mostly, changing jobs often and not making much money, which he blamed on his lack of education.

Dad was indecisive and managed to avoid responsibility by letting Mom handle everything—which she did well. Dad was good at spending money, though, leaving it to Mom to juggle expenses to make ends meet.

Personality-wise, Mom was a stoic, even an unfeeling type of parent. As I recall, she never showed any physical attention to me or my siblings, and seldom spoke to any of us at length. I don't remember ever sitting down with her for a mother-daughter chat. She was absent to us, like a ghostly figure who never really revealed herself.

My dad gave us attention but always in an appraising sort of way. He would remark about how we looked—nice or otherwise. He never kept his comments to himself. If it looked like we had lost or gained weight, he would always let us know. His remarks were particularly painful while I was in my chubby stage.

"Julie is really solid," he'd say, and then invite the person who was visiting to lift me up, like I was a weight to challenge someone's strength.

"Pleasingly plump, isn't she?" he'd chuckle.

Another time when I was playing on the floor with my brother and sister, he said that I was "as broad as a barn door."

He would compare me to my sister who was "thin as a rail."

It was all very hurtful. The three of us were extremely close. Maybe we banded together because of how we were treated by our parents. We were everything to each other. We were the family. We took care of each other emotionally, being supportive and helping one another through difficult times by telling jokes and laughing.

We thought it was normal that our parents spent all their free time having friends over or going to friends' houses. We thought it was normal that our parents consumed a case of beer over a weekend and a couple of six-packs during the week, or even more if there was a party. They were never stumbling, falling-down drunks; they just drank a lot.

We thought it was normal that our parents didn't have much time for us. We were simply not a priority to them. Although we were looked after in terms of food, shelter, and clothing, we were deprived of their love. Their needs came first.

They both smoked heavily. I hated it and told them so. It was horrid to live in a house that was always filled with smoke. I was always emptying overflowing ashtrays. My parents didn't care how anyone else felt about their actions, least of all me.

I knew my mother was not happy being married to my father. Dad, though he was never treated for it, suffered from a manic-depressive disorder. His moods were volatile. He would fly into a rage at the drop of a hat. Mom, usually so cool and level headed, would respond to his rages by bursting into tears and running to her bedroom.

This type of scene was repeated many times throughout our childhood. Of course, there was no explanation to us about what was happening. We just sat there, watching and worrying.

Julie

As the oldest child, many expectations were heaped on me. I was housekeeper, cook, and baby sitter, but I got nothing in return. I did get to take piano lessons for five years, though, from the nuns at St. Michael's. Whenever I would feel lonely or frustrated, I would play the piano. It was such a great comfort and release for me!

My best childhood memories involve my grandparents. I was very close to all four of them. I knew they liked having me visit at their homes. My mother's parents in particular made me feel wonderful. They lived in a rural dairy community about twenty miles from us and had a weathered old country home with a veranda that wrapped all around the house.

Grandfather had been a blacksmith and Grandmother had stayed home to raise six children. They were the soul of love and solid character.

I remember spending hours in the garden with Grandfather. I felt so small among the looming rows of corn. I can still smell the ripe tomatoes. His crops were magnificent. We would pick the vegetables and carry them in bushel baskets to Grandmother, who always seemed to be in the kitchen.

I loved watching Grandmother work. She used the same big blue bowl and the same utensils every day. She was so methodical as she pared the potatoes and prepared the rest of the meal. I became mesmerized by the ritual of her movements and her sureness around the kitchen. It was like a beautiful and graceful dance.

After lunch we played checkers, cards, or Scrabble. They never rushed. I felt such joy at being with these two people who had all the time in the world —just for me.

Grade school was difficult for me at first. I was a very chubby child, and kids love to torment anyone different. After the others got to know me, though, I ended up having a large circle of friends.

I knew I was well liked, which gave me confidence. I was voted president of my class every year. All my teachers loved me. They knew they could depend on me to take charge of the class or do any extra work that needed to be done. I enjoyed the attention and the role of leader.

When I was thirteen, my parents bought the only house we ever owned. It was right across the street from our rented house and like a dream come true for me. The new house was a huge Victorian-style with ten big rooms and two bathrooms.

The wealthy man who had owned the house left us some of the furnishings. There were beautifully ornamented lamps and antique handcrafted wooden furniture. The small lot was professionally landscaped with trees, shrubs, and a lovely rose garden in back.

I had never known such grandeur! I had never been so happy as when we moved into that house.

About a year later, in 1965, I started changing physically, and the changes were quite rapid. I grew taller, lost my chubby shape and became a well-developed, attractive teenager. I had shoulder-length brown hair with red highlights. Every night I set my hair in those huge brush rollers we used to use, to take out its natural wave, because the straight look was popular then. I wore only a little mascara. I really didn't need makeup because I had one of those peaches-and-cream complexions, except in summer when I'd get freckles.

In high school, people thought I had a great smile. Those teen years were wonderful. I was on the student council, played basketball and sang in the choir. It was the first time in my life that I felt good about how I looked. The boys took notice of me right away. I couldn't get enough attention or compliments. I felt a sense of power. It was a feeling of self worth that I had never experienced before.

Since my parents never talked with me much about anything, of course they never talked to me about sex. Mom seemed quite concerned when I started dating, but she never gave me information about the feelings that can happen between a boy and a girl. She never informed me about contraception. I guess she believed that I would just somehow be a "good girl."

She didn't know that I had been involved in some fairly heavy petting since about eighth grade. I was happy with just petting and assumed my boyfriends were, too.

When I was fifteen, I started being pursued by Jim, who was a senior. Although his brazen behavior and public show of interest in me were a little intimidating, I was flattered by the attention. I liked what I thought were his strong work ethic and decision-making skills. I thought he was sensible and stable.

Julie

After about five months of dating, Jim demanded that we have sex, threatening to leave me if I refused. I couldn't face the thought of life without him, so I reluctantly gave in.

Julie

We were lucky for a year, but in late June 1967, I realized I was pregnant. I couldn't believe this was happening to me! I was on the student council and the basketball team. I wanted to go to college and become a teacher. It was all over for me, that summer before the start of my junior year. Intellectually, I knew this, but I tried not to think about it.

Jim had graduated and was signed up to enter the navy in August. I remember the evening I told Jim about my condition. We were watching the movie *Alfie* at our local theater when I started to cry. Jim asked me why I was crying, and I said, "Because I'm pregnant!"

We went to have Cokes and talk about it. Neither of us had any idea of what to do. So we did nothing. He left for the navy, and I got ready to start school.

I didn't look pregnant, and even though I was sick every morning getting ready for school, I just pushed it all to the back of my mind and pretended that none of it was happening.

When I was about five months along, my clothes started fitting a little snugly. One Saturday before my dad came home from work, I walked into the kitchen and found Mom sitting at the kitchen table, as if she had been waiting for me. When she blurted out something about my not having a period and could I be pregnant, I replied, "Yes."

She started crying and saying hurtful things like, "We never thought that you, the perfect student, the good child, would end up like this!"

Then she dropped the bombshell, telling me that I had been born out of wedlock. I couldn't believe it! She had been twenty-one years old, and Dad had been in the service.

I also found out that my mother didn't even raise me for the first two years of my life—I had lived with her parents until Dad got out of the service. All of a sudden, I understood why I had always felt such a sense of closeness to those grandparents.

As if that wasn't enough, she went on to tell me another family secret—that my dad's sister had given birth to a child out of wedlock and placed him for adoption. She sure chose a great time to tell me all of that!

When she was finished with me, I was overwhelmed. I left the house and started walking toward our church, which was a block away. I was a devout Catholic and felt the need to go to confession, to confess my sin.

The priest was so kind and understanding. He made me feel much better. As I was on my way back home, I noticed that my dad was walking toward the church looking for me. He came up to me and just hugged me. He didn't say a word. Somehow he must have known how I needed that. Without talking, he had finally let me know that he loved me.

I didn't know it then, but the priest's reactions and Dad's unspoken love had to hold me for a long, long time.

My mother took me to the family doctor, I think with the idea of abortion in mind. The doctor said it was too late—that I was three months along and too far gone. The doctor was wrong—I was five months along. But what difference did it make?

Mom and Dad put their heads together and decided to send me off to live with my aunt. When that plan fell through, they came up with another. At 11:00 P.M. one night, Dad woke me up to tell me that all of us except him would be moving to Arizona. We would stay with my uncle until after I had the baby.

My opinion was never sought in any of this planning. No one asked me how I felt about these decisions. But at that point, I was relieved that someone else was handling the problem.

In November 1967, Mom, Joseph, Stephanie, and I began our drive from Vermont to Arizona. We told everyone that my parents were having marital problems and they were separating for a while. Other than our immediate family, nobody knew the real truth. Jim didn't tell his family. I never told even one friend.

Julie

I was confused, frightened and worried. What would happen to my body during the pregnancy and labor? What about afterwards—what would my body be like when it was over? Where would I go to school? Where would we live? What would happen to my child?

Mom never talked about any of this with me, and I was too ashamed to ask. I felt bad for letting myself get into this predicament. I should have been smarter. I felt guilty for putting my brother and sister through the trauma of moving away from our lovely home. I felt awful about all the arrangements my parents had to make financially, and for Mom having to quit her job. Most of all, I felt so alone!

We arrived at my uncle's home in Tucson, tired and irritable. He lived in a fairly large house with his wife and eight children.

It was the first time we had met our cousins. They weren't very friendly to us, so there was no companionship to be found there. With four more people, it was a little crowded too. But the worst part was that no one ever mentioned my condition.

It didn't take Mom long to find a job in a nearby hospital. She located an apartment and enrolled us in school. Coming from a small town, I found the high school intimidating. It was the size of a college campus! Kids from our part of the city had to begin classes at 6:00 A.M.

My mother formed a car pool with other parents in our apartment complex, and they took turns driving us to and from school. I was exhausted by the time I got home from classes at 12:30. All I could do was drop into bed for a nap.

I was expanding quickly and had no maternity clothes, so I wore a trench coat to school in an attempt to hide my condition. Fortunately baggy dresses were in style, so I still had a few clothes that fit, but I was running out of things to wear and Mom didn't seem to care.

In December, Dad came from Vermont for a Christmas get-together. It was really nice to see him. I was almost eight months pregnant and Mom had finally bought me two maternity outfits. That was all I had to wear. Mom seemed happier while Dad was there. It was a strange Christmas but good to be together again.

One day, within weeks of when I was due to deliver, I was called into the principal's office and told that I was expelled from school for being pregnant. Pregnant girls were not allowed in school, and I was to call my mother to come get me.

I was so humiliated! I was in tears when Mom arrived. She took me home without a word of comfort. Just her cold silence as usual.

The following week she took me to a special school for unwed mothers. Even though I ended up only being there for two weeks, it was the one place I felt I belonged. We were all going through the same thing, and that felt comfortable. Plus, classes were held at a reasonable hour, so I didn't have to get up so early!

It was January before Mom took me to a doctor again. Even though she was a registered nurse, she had not taken me for any prenatal care. The doctor examined me, then admonished me for putting my family through this ordeal. There were no words of consolation for me. He acted as though I had the plague, muttering something about why is it that the pretty and smart girls always seem to end up like this. I hated the man.

One day in February, although I wasn't sure at first, my labor started. I had spent many hours in the school library trying to learn about labor and delivery, so I had a little knowledge. Neither my doctor nor my mother told me anything about what to expect.

I didn't tell Mom about the pains when she left for work at 2:30 that afternoon. But by 7:30 I had to have Stephanie call Mom and ask her to come home.

Mom arrived home, a little upset because I hadn't mentioned anything to her before she had left for work. Off we went to the hospital—a different one than the hospital where Mom worked. I don't remember Mom saying good-bye to me at the hospital. I just remember her being gone. I guess she went back to work.

They took me to a labor room and the pains began in earnest. I remember thinking how unpleasant and painful it all was. By about 9:30 P.M., my doctor arrived and broke my water. Then things went really fast, and the pain became intense.

Julie

There was no sympathy or encouragement from anyone. I don't believe the doctor even spoke to me. Once, when I moaned aloud in pain, the nurse scolded me, saying, "All that noise won't make the pain any easier, you know."

At about 10:00 P.M., I was taken to the delivery room, a gas mask was placed over my face, and everything went dark. When I awoke, I was in a private room in the hospital. Mom was standing nearby looking worried, but I don't remember her saying a word to me.

I was not allowed to see my baby. The nurses wouldn't even tell me if I had a girl or a boy! Finally, the next day, the doctor told me that I had a son who weighed seven pounds, one ounce. That's all I knew about him for twenty-five years.

My parents made the decision that my son would be adopted by a loving two-parent family. That was it—no discussion. I was seventeen and had been told that I could not finish school while raising a child, so it seemed for the best. At the time, I had no idea how losing my child would impact the rest of my life.

After signing papers in the hospital, I cried and cried. A nurse came in and whisked my mother out of the room, saying I needed time alone. Again, no one was there to comfort me. I left the hospital the next day, and two weeks later we were all on our way back to Vermont.

I felt empty—as if I had left part of myself in Arizona. No one talked to me about this because no one outside the family knew, and no one in the family would even discuss it. I couldn't even talk to Stephanie about it. We had always talked about everything, but the whole subject became taboo even to think about, much less talk about.

I went back to my old high school three months before the end of the school year and graduated the following year. It was a time of emptiness and loneliness. My whole attitude about life had changed. I was no longer interested in anything—not even basketball. The spirit that had made me a leader was gone. I floated along in kind of a dream state.

Jim was still in the service while I was finishing high school, so I took advantage of his absence to date other people. I was horrified by the changes the pregnancy had caused to my body. It was obvious that I would never be the same again.

I had been so proud of my body just two years before, but now I viewed myself with loathing and disgust. Attention from males helped me feel better about myself. I wasn't promiscuous, but I needed men to be sexually attracted to me in order to feel whole.

Even though my parents had forbidden me to see him, Jim and I started dating again when he was discharged from the navy. He eventually came to my house and asked their permission! I had always admired this forthright quality in him. My parents relented.

Jim and I started having sex again, still without contraception. I have no idea why we ventured into those dangerous waters again! After a few "false alarms," during which I became very panicky, we decided we should get married and became formally engaged. I felt like I had to stay with Jim because he was the father of my child. He was the only bond I had with my son.

Because our family didn't have enough money for me to go to college, I opted for a two-year medical secretary course. After graduation, I commuted to classes, not wanting to live on campus because I didn't want to be apart from Jim. I knew I would be tempted to see other men if I stayed on campus. As it happened, I did see other men, but I never pursued anything long-term with any of them.

Jim and I married in 1971, three years after our first son was born. I always felt as though something was missing from our relationship. Nevertheless, after three years of marriage, we decided to start a family.

Kim was born in 1975 when I was twenty-four, and about three years later we had our son, Jamie. The children helped fill the void in my life, and heaven knows, they kept me busy!

While I was on maternity leave with Kim, I saw a Phil Donohue show about adoptees who were searching for their birth parents. Something about that show convinced me that I would find my son. I wanted desperately to let him know that he had always been loved.

I contacted a search organization, paid a membership fee and received a very skimpy guide about how to conduct a search. I tried to read it but got totally confused. I put the guide away and didn't do anything else about it for years.

Julie

My marriage was still not satisfying to me. Jim worked endless hours and was never home to help with the kids. It was frustrating to work full time myself, and then come to home to the burden of raising children alone and keeping house. I sometimes thought I would go over the edge.

While I was pregnant with Jamie, Mom was living with us temporarily. She was dying of lung cancer. During my entire pregnancy, she was receiving radiation treatments and declining rapidly. It was extra work for me, but I figured it was my duty.

My mother died when Jamie was eight months old. It was a terribly depressing time. Mom and I never did manage to discuss my first son's birth or any of what had happened. Now we will never be able to discuss anything.

The next year, Dad lost his job. He and Mom had been separated since she got sick, and he'd been drinking very heavily. He was only in his early fifties at the time, but he never worked again.

I believe he eventually quit drinking, but his severe depression and self-centered attitude keep us apart to this day. He only wants to talk about himself. It is nearly impossible to have a two-way conversation with him. Dad and I rarely see each other, and he's really not a part of my life.

There were many times when I thought I should leave my husband. He had become very much like my father, with uncontrolled mood swings and depression. I hated the mind games he kept playing. There were times he would refuse to talk to me. Once, three months went by without him speaking to me.

I didn't have the courage to leave. I wasn't financially secure and didn't want to be poor, so I stayed. We tried counseling, but he never felt that he had a problem. He said any problems we had were mine.

By 1990, things got really bad. The business that Jim and his brother-in-law owned burned to the ground. We went through a dreadful time—suing the insurance company and then never recovering the money we should have. Jim had to get a job at two-thirds of his former salary, and our lifestyle changed dramatically. He became more depressed, and so did I.

I sought counseling for myself, which began a two-year period of working through my issues, especially the birth and loss of my first son. Jim never seemed to share my deep feelings about our son. This was the first time I had been able to explain my sadness to someone who understood, and it took so much energy to bring all that out!

Eventually I went from individual counseling to a group with four other women. I was finally able to tell my story and hear people's reactions. I started to feel like I was recovering and finding myself again.

Since 1992 I've continued to come to terms with my losses. I have learned to grieve, and then move on.

I never stopped thinking about my first son. I think the healing I experienced in counseling gave me the strength to start my search. I wrote for the hospital records and found the name of the lawyer who had handled the adoption.

When I sent a letter to him, I received a curt reply that he had died. When I requested information about the records, I was told they'd been destroyed. I contacted the lawyer's wife to see if she could help, but a secretary wrote back saying not to bother her with this. I later found out that this lawyer had been my son's godfather!

I was stymied. I found out about another search organization and located a contact person in Arizona. This woman worked in a state office and had access to adoption records in a card file. I called her, and she was able to get the information in front of her, but said that she couldn't tell me anything. But she did tell me that his name was Kenneth. I finally had a name to call my son.

Several months and many phone calls later, she mailed me some non-identifying information. I received the package at work and almost collapsed when I opened it.

What a joyful surprise! There were four photos of Kenneth when he was little! Now I had a face to put with the name. It was like being in shock. Here in front of me, in these pictures, was my son.

I called Jim at work to tell him but couldn't even speak through my tears. I tried to express the happiness and relief I felt just at seeing those pictures. I didn't feel that Jim understood, but I think he was happy for me.

Yet another search group in Phoenix helped with the remainder of the process of finding my son. There were many layers of information to uncover and piece together. My sister and I spent many hours at libraries going through various documents.

We ended up finding Kenneth's family through names of men in northern Arizona who were connected to a particular church. Searching the church records, we found a man and his wife with a son named Kenneth who was born in 1968. Bingo!

I was almost positive that this was my son—but how to make contact? I was going to write a letter, but my search team suggested that a phone call would be best. They were right. After all this searching, I really needed to know—now.

On May 7, 1993, at about 9:15 P.M. eastern time, I called the Arizona number where I thought Kenneth lived. A woman answered. That threw me —I was expecting him to answer. She sounded older, so it probably wasn't his wife. I assumed it was his adoptive mother.

"My name is Julie O'Grady," I told her. "I gave birth to your son Kenneth in 1968."

She sort of gasped, but then began to thank me for giving them such a wonderful son—going on and on about what a great guy he was, so articulate and what gorgeous eyes he had. I asked her some questions, especially about what he looked like now, since the only pictures I'd seen were when he was little.

She described him to me. She said Kenneth was twenty-five years old, six feet tall, had bluish-gray eyes, blonde hair, and had graduated from a college in California with a degree in history and video production. I asked as many questions as I dared, then asked where he lived. She wouldn't tell me or give me his phone number. But she promised to contact him and let him know I wanted to speak with him. I also made her promise she wouldn't leave me dangling for days—that if he didn't want to talk to me, she'd call me right away.

Kenneth called the next day. It was the day before Mother's Day. His voice sounded very gentle and low, and there was a degree of excitement in it, too. I started to cry, so I asked him to please give me a couple of minutes to collect myself. Then we talked for about thirty minutes. I told him about his family in Vermont, the circumstances of his being adopted, and how I found him.

He was amazed at all I had gone through to find him. He had thought of searching too but had no idea where to start. He also wanted to make sure that I had the right person. That made me chuckle. I knew he was my son.

Kenneth told me that he lived in Chicago now, and his main occupation was playing in a heavy metal-type band called "Angst." His dream was to make it big time in the music world. In the meantime, he was supplementing his income as a bar manager at a downtown cafe. I thought it strange that his adoptive mother never mentioned the band.

Kenneth went on to say that the band might be playing in New York that July, and maybe we could meet then. I was excited and frightened. Would he like me? What kinds of things would I find out about him when I actually got to know him?

I needn't have worried because that meeting never happened. The band didn't get the job in New York. Time just kept rolling by with little contact initiated by Kenneth. In the past few years I have received maybe three letters and two phone calls. The rest of the time I have done the contacting.

My family was happy to hear I had found my son. Jamie, who was sixteen, was most enthusiastic about having an older brother. Kim, however, wasn't as excited and told Jamie that she couldn't picture Ken as part of our family, and that he would never be a real brother to Jamie. Jim was quietly supportive, but had no desire to speak with Ken on the phone or write to him. I couldn't quite understand that, since Jim was his father.

In the summer of 1994, I decided that the only way to have closure to my search was to see him in person. He clearly had no intention of making a trip to Vermont, even if I sent him an airline ticket. So I asked if we could come visit him. I was surprised that he seemed excited about the idea.

On October 5, 1994, my sister Stephanie, my son Jamie, and I made the trip to Chicago to meet Ken. He and his girlfriend Tessie were right at the bottom of the ramp as we came off the plane. There was no time to put down our bags and take a photo, but the picture of his face at that moment is indelibly printed in my mind.

My first feelings were a little odd. Here was my son, my child, a stranger. He seemed smaller than I had imagined him but so beautiful. His gentleness and nervousness were evident as we left the airport and drove into the city.

120

Julie

I kept trying to memorize everything about him, without letting him know that I was staring. I'm sure I was not as discreet as I tried to be. He dropped us off at our hotel and then went home to change for dinner. I think he just needed a little time away from the intensity of the situation.

Ken was having a hard time relaxing with us. He seemed most comfortable the day before we left, when the two of us were going through the family photo album I had brought along for him. It was an emotional three days, and I was a little frustrated that we didn't have as much time together as I had hoped. He had to work all day Friday and edit a video with the band at night.

After traveling so far, I got to see him so little. And I was still unable to get him to commit to a Vermont visit.

I had fantasized that this meeting would help integrate Kenneth into our lives, and that contact with him would be more ongoing. But it hasn't happened that way. Ken told me that he needs space to sort out his feelings about being found, and he wants me to be patient with him. I'm trying to be patient, but I desperately want him as part of my family. He is my son.

Julie, her birth son, and son

I sent Kenneth's adoptive mother, Sharon, a short letter, telling her how fortunate Ken was to have been placed in such a warm family and that he had told me many good things about her. I invited her to get to know me and ask me questions if she wanted. I said that I hoped we would get to know each other and maybe be friends some day. That letter received no response.

At Christmas, I sent another card and letter, telling her that I understood if she was uneasy about all of this, but I assured her that we only wanted to give Kenneth our love and in no way meant to usurp her position as his parent. No response.

I knew that Ken's adoptive parents had divorced about a year before, so I assumed Sharon was going through some emotional upheaval. I thought I'd try the adoptive father. I sent him a letter with similar messages. No response from him, either.

This makes me angry. What can they possibly fear from me? I live 1,200 miles from Kenneth and twice as far from them. I have no power to undo the past—no power to threaten their parental roles. But apparently, they have no desire to know me or my family. I gave them my child, and they refuse to even acknowledge me.

Meanwhile, life goes on. Jim is forty-six and in the car business, which he hates. He actually works at the same job as my father. Ironic, isn't it? Jim is frustrated and depressed a lot of the time. Our relationship is far from perfect. It is difficult to find a common ground, as he doesn't share many of my interests. But our marriage is not totally negative by any means.

Jim has always tried to be a good husband and provider. And I have to own part of our problems as well. The experience of losing Kenneth made me a different person than I would have been—and I have my own demons to deal with around that issue. I have not always been the easiest person to live with, either.

I continue to work at the university as a technical secretary in the medical field—at the same type of job since my marriage in 1971. Because of the tuition remission policy, I've been able to afford a college education for Kim and Jamie. The work isn't very challenging, but I've been taking classes with the goal of finishing my four-year degree. I'm not sure where this will lead me, but I've always wanted to teach—maybe in adult education.

Julie

It was only after finding my son that I was able to progress with my ambitions. I am regaining the confidence I lost so long ago and can pursue my own dreams. The whole search experience set me free from the dark hole I had been buried in. It has been an emotional cleansing.

I feel more secure about myself now and am slowly getting rid of the guilt about the past. I am feeling less like a teenage girl who shamed her family and more like the strong and worthwhile woman I am.

There are still many unanswered questions where Ken is concerned. He has become a kind of obsession with me. I think about him and worry about him every day. I wonder what he is feeling about me. I have decided that this compulsive behavior needs to stop. I need to stop getting bogged down with worrying about what he will or will not do about our relationship. I will never abandon him again, but I need to have a clear space in my mind. I need to let him go and decide for himself if he wants to be part of our lives.

Painful as it is, I have decided not to initiate further contact with my son. I can't be the only person in the relationship willing to make a commitment. I will send gifts and a letter on Christmas and his birthday but will not try to force anything. I can't have this relationship alone. He needs to want me, too. I will continue to wait for him.

* * *

Chapter Nine

๑ *Evie* ๑

The oldest of four children, I was an insecure little girl with a lot of health problems because of "nervousness" as the doctors called it. After my dear grampa died when I was four, my mom was the only person who could calm my nerves. Unfortunately, when she and my dad would start drinking, any feelings of safety and security immediately turned to fear.

My dad worked hard and became a very successful businessman. Proud of having been a boxer in the navy, my dad was tall, handsome, aggressive and had a bad temper. All of the kids were afraid of him—especially when he drank. We loved him, too, and really wanted to please him. Mom always told me, "Keep the kids quiet so your dad doesn't get mad." But he seemed to get mad anyway, no matter how hard I tried to control the kids.

I felt it was my duty to "keep the monster happy" and I tried to make him feel better. I had this notion that if I could somehow keep peace in the family, my parents wouldn't drink, and then we'd all be happy like the Cleavers on TV.

When I was very young, my dad would come to me in my bed and hurt me in ways I never talked about. After he stopped doing that, he came into bed with me and just cried and cried about his life. He suffered a lot from having been abandoned as a child and had hoped our family would be the perfect one he never had.

My mom was an Irish beauty, and my dad liked to show her off to friends. I never understood how he could be so proud of her and still flirt with other women and be sexual with them. My dad liked to flirt with anything in a skirt and turned most conversations into something sexual. Watching other women around my dad made me sick to my stomach. I used to wish I wasn't a girl because then I wouldn't have to be thin, beautiful and sexy.

I was dependent on my mom to make life feel normal. When she was having a good day, everything was fine. But when she had a bad day, it usually included a migraine headache. I remember sitting next to her when she was sick or drunk to make sure she didn't stop breathing. I was terribly afraid that she would die and leave me and my younger siblings alone with my dad.

My mom and dad broke up and got back together again several times while I was a child. Every time he would move out, we were so happy, and it was like a weight was lifted from our lives. But then he came back and everything started again. The drinking got worse and worse.

When my dad had his after-work drinks, Mom usually joined him. I hated it when she was drunk because her whole personality changed. Usually she was very demure—very private and uptight about sexual things. But when she was drinking, she acted all feminine and flirty with other men. Then my dad would get possessive, yell at her, and there'd be a big fight.

I went to a large public school in a suburb of Minneapolis. After school, I'd hurry home to make sure Mom was still there. I was always afraid she'd go away forever some day.

I hated being young and wanted to grow up as quickly as possible. But I was quite shy about boys. When I was thirteen, I told my mom, "Eeew! I don't ever want a boy to touch me."

My mom said, "Don't worry. This is just a phase, and you'll get over it."

I did become very interested in boys. I thought about them all the time. But when a boy first tried to kiss me, I was disgusted. I realized that I was terrified of being alone with a man—especially an older man. I desperately wanted a boyfriend like everyone else, but the thought of kissing a boy or being touched by one repulsed me, and I didn't know why. I wanted to get over this silly thing about boys and find Mr. Right. We would get married, have children and everything would be wonderful.

My parents began to worry that there was something wrong with me, and sent me to therapy. The only conclusion the counselor could make was that I had an inferiority complex and would eventually grow out of it. Sexual abuse was never mentioned, as I had completely blocked it out by that time.

Mom thought modeling school might help me overcome my shyness and groom me for being a woman. I believed that, if I was pretty like my mom, my life would be perfect. No matter how hard I worked at being beautiful, I couldn't seem to lose weight. I guess I take after my dad's German side of the family. The effort made me hate the pressures of being a girl even more than before.

Then something very good happened. When I was fourteen, my parents joined Alcoholics Anonymous. Life at home became sane for the first time, and my parents started getting along well. I didn't have much trust in anything by then, but I pretended things were good and shoved all the pain away.

Evie

I kept the same group of friends throughout high school. I had boyfriends and even went steady in eleventh and twelfth grade. Although the guys were very nice, I was still afraid to be alone with them—and would do just about anything to make sure that didn't happen.

In preparation for college, I went on a diet, was fitted for contact lenses and bleached my hair. Mom bought me all new clothes and I felt like hot stuff. On the outside I looked good, and I believed that was what mattered.

In 1966, when I was still eighteen, I met Les at the drive-in. He was a fry cook, and I was a car-hop. Les was cute and loved to party. He paid a lot of attention to me, and I fell in love. I was sure this was Mr. Right.

There were two things about which I was adamant. I was never going to drink alcohol, and I was going to remain a virgin until marriage. I wouldn't go all the way with Les even though I loved him. This created quite a problem in our relationship because Les wanted to have sex, and I kept saying no.

Two weeks before college started, Les broke up with me because, as he put it, "I wasn't ready to grow up." He said he wanted to find himself a real woman. That's exactly what he said to me. I couldn't believe he could be so heartless. I was convinced that my whole survival was about finding a husband and being a good wife and mother.

Needless to say, the experience with Les made me more confused and depressed than ever. I spent a lot of time crying into my pillow and threatened to cancel my plans for the university. My mother said, "Don't worry. It'll all turn out for the best."

I started college. After all, it was something to do until I met the real Mr. Right. Within two weeks, a very handsome man from my history class asked me to go to the homecoming dance with him. I was thrilled. I remember thinking that he must be "The One," and that's why Les had broken up with me—so I could meet Lonny. It was destiny.

The night of the dance, when Lonny asked me what I wanted to drink, I thought, "I'm not going to make the same mistake twice," fearing that I would lose him, too. So I said, "I'll have whatever you're drinking."

That night changed my life forever. Just one drink made me feel confident and beautiful. I loved it. I guess I eventually blacked out. I don't remember anything else—what we did, or even if we went to the dance.

About a month later, I lost my virginity. I had such tremendous guilt about being sexual. I felt like soiled goods and was sure no one would ever want to marry me. I still had all the feelings of disgust and rage about being touched and had to be drunk in order to have sex. I tried to be in love with Lonny, but I couldn't deal with the shame. Not knowing what else to do, I ended the relationship. Booze was slowly becoming my best friend.

I thought about birth control, but I figured I didn't need it. Two different doctors had told me that I would probably never have children. I only had one or two periods a year, and they assumed I was sterile. Besides, using birth control would mean that I was sexual, and I could barely admit that to myself.

The first time I saw Ralph, I was instantly attracted to him. He was tall, dark and handsome with an arrogant edge that enticed me. I played all the coy and flirty games I knew whenever our paths crossed. Within two weeks, he asked me out.

Ralph also came from an alcoholic family. He was a lot like my dad—very strong and controlling. My physical appearance seemed to be his main focal point, and I was never quite as thin or pretty as he wanted me to be. Ralph had been abused as a child, and I felt like he needed me to take care of him. It was good to be needed.

We had been dating for about a year when Ralph asked me to marry him. He told me he had worked it all out in his head, and I would become a flight attendant to put him through law school. He would make tons of money, and we could have a house full of kids.

I remember thinking, "My happiness is just around the corner!" Two months later I found out I was pregnant. I couldn't believe this could happen. The doctors had been wrong! How could I be having a baby? I felt like a baby myself. I was beginning to feel out of control with my drinking, yet I wasn't ready to give it up. It was all a terrible mess, and I didn't know what to do.

When I told my mom about the pregnancy, she yelled at me and called me a tramp and a slut. Even though I'd been calling myself those names for a long time, it really hurt to have my mom say them. At the same time, it was almost a relief that she knew the truth about me.

My mom said, "How could you do this? This will break your father's heart!" And when my mom told him, he actually cried. Big, sad tears. Watching him cry, I felt cold and sick inside, like the scum of the earth.

Ralph wanted to marry me. We went to a couple of pre-marital counseling sessions at my church, but it was clear that I just could not do "what was right." Ralph was crushed. My parents were devastated. I was appalled by all the turns my life was taking.

I was forbidden to see Ralph again. It was decided that I would go to California and stay with friends of the family. I told everyone that I was transferring to Stanford University. I couldn't tell the truth because being an unwed mother in 1968 was completely unacceptable. My dad arranged for an address in Los Angeles so Ralph could write me and send money.

Evie

Horribly lonely and depressed, I bought a wedding band at Woolworth's to cover my shame. I told everyone I met that my husband was away in Vietnam. The only people who knew the real story were the people with whom I stayed, my parents, one of my brothers, and my best friend. I lived that lie the whole time I was in California.

Ralph graduated from the university and joined the army. He wrote often, sending money whenever he could. He tried to be supportive but it was never enough for me. I took out my pain and anger on Ralph, raging at him in my letters. It was all his fault! I hated being away from my family and friends. I hated being like this. I hated the whole stinking mess and didn't know how to deal with it except to drink my feelings away. I did try to take it easy on my drinking, though, for the baby's sake.

I had to help pay for my medical expenses, so I found a series of baby-sitting jobs in different parts of the Bay Area. One of my jobs was in San Jose, baby sitting for two boys whose mother had died. I commuted almost an hour each way to handle the cooking, cleaning, and laundry for the boys and their dad.

One evening as I was getting ready to leave for home, the dad suddenly came out of the bedroom naked. I was shocked. He began saying things like, "I know what kind of girl you are. You can have it if you want it."

I almost threw up. In fact, I wish I had—all over him. I grabbed my coat and left, never to return. I wondered if this was the kind of treatment I deserved. I wasn't sure.

Shortly after that experience, one of my doctors took me aside and told me of a very nice couple that would be willing to pay me $25,000 for my baby. No amount of money was enough to pay for my baby. If I had to give him up, I wanted him to be a gift to someone. I felt very strongly about that.

Much of that time away from home seemed like a nightmare. Still, there was a part of me that absolutely loved being pregnant. I loved the feeling of a life inside me, at the same time feeling guilty about being happy. I always felt a strong connection with my baby. I am convinced it is some kind of psychic connection.

I knew he was a boy. Every day I would rub my belly with cocoa butter and talk to him, saying, "You are a special baby and I love you very much. I won't be able to raise you myself, but you will have another mother who will love you. Remember, I will always, always love you. And some day we will come back together again."

I knew I would have to say good-bye to my baby—and I knew just as surely that we would meet again some day. Because of my dad's sad childhood, I wanted to make sure my son had a good start. I kept telling him how special he was.

A week before my baby was due, my mom flew out to California to be with me. I ended up being six weeks overdue. Frustrated, the doctor told me I needed to let go of my baby—that I didn't want to give birth to him because I didn't want to lose him.

"You can't keep him inside you forever," he said. "You have to let him go." I knew that, but my body couldn't do it. My mom and I became closer during that time. I remember we talked a lot and spent quiet times just being together.

When I finally went into labor, I was as big as a house. The birthing process was long and difficult. I lost a great deal of blood. Immediately afterwards I couldn't even stand on my own. Mom pushed my wheel chair down to the nursery so I could see my baby, but every time I saw him I would start to faint from weakness. I only remember a little red face in a blue blanket and the odor of smelling salts the nurse held under my nose. I never held my baby.

Those days in the hospital were the most painful days of my life, both physically and emotionally. I was so sore that ice packs and heating lamps were on me most of the time. All I could do was lie there and cry. The nurses had tucked me away in a corner of the ward so I wouldn't upset the other mothers. They were nice enough to put a "Mrs." on my chart, so that nobody would know that I was an unwed mother.

One morning a new nurse helped me into the shower, promising to bring my baby as soon as I was finished. I started to cry and told her "I'm not allowed to see my baby because I'm not married and I'm giving him up." She let go of me immediately. I slumped to the shower floor and laid there sobbing until I had enough strength to drag myself back to bed.

I tried to imagine raising my son but I couldn't. My father, maybe because of his own feelings of abandonment, wanted me to bring him home. My mother told me if I kept the baby I couldn't come home again. Ralph wanted custody, saying his mother would raise the baby, but I didn't think she had done such a good job with Ralph and wanted my baby to have a clean start.

I hated making the decision. It was the most difficult thing I've ever done. But I placed my baby son, whom I named Richard Andrew Bennett, for adoption in November 1968, just two days after his birth. Then I went to the airport and got on a plane for Minneapolis.

I arrived at home sixty pounds heavier than when I had left for "college." Everything seemed so bleak. I was still a mess physically, too. I stayed in my room for weeks and cried a lot. My mom and dad tried to get me out of my depression, but nothing seemed to work. Except alcohol. That seemed to make me feel better. I tried going out with my old friends, but I felt more distant from them than ever. So I drank even more. I dyed my hair black and started wearing glasses again, trying to make myself as unattractive to men as possible.

I eventually got a job as a night manager at a restaurant and lost the extra weight I had been carrying around. I looked great. That was the biggest lie of all because I was such a mess on the inside, starting with the gaping hole that was caused by missing my baby. It was a secret hole, and it isolated me from everyone—even myself. Nothing could fill it. Not men, not drugs, not alcohol. But alcohol helped. Or so I thought.

I was on a downhill slide between the ages of twenty and twenty-four. I worked occasionally, went to school from time to time, but couldn't seem to focus on anything. I was involved in a car accident and started taking valium for chronic pain. It was also during this time that my parents divorced. My mother had remained sober, but my father had started drinking again.

People started telling me that I was an alcoholic. My girlfriends said I got insane when I was drunk, and even my doctor was worried that I was suicidal and suggested that I had "a problem." One day I couldn't take it any more and called Alcoholics Anonymous, which saved my life.

After my pregnancy, my "female problems" returned. Cysts began to grow on my ovaries. One thing led to another and at twenty-nine, I had to have a hysterectomy.

Drunk or sober, I always had trouble with men. I was in and out of therapy. I guess, considering my background, it's only natural that I'd have trouble trusting, would fear intimacy, and so forth. Ralph and I got back together and broke up several times after the baby was born. We couldn't seem to let each other go.

I had other short relationships with a lot of men.

I got married when I was thirty-five to a sweet guy who was nine years younger than I. Maybe one of the reasons we ended up divorced four years later was that I mothered him. I took care of Johnny totally, even taking responsibility for his emotions.

Call it intuition or extra sensory perception—but I always felt close to my baby, even though we weren't together. And I always knew I would see him again. I remember looking at all the babies in the mall to see if I recognized any of them. For years I looked at all the little boys who were his age. In search of a support system, I called some adoption agencies and located a group of women who had also given their babies up for adoption.

We met regularly, sharing our feelings and experiences. We also spoke to high school and church groups about what unwed pregnancy is really like. That group helped heal my emotional scars more than all the therapy I had undergone over the years.

But I still battled depression. It hit me especially hard at Thanksgiving, which was near his birthday. I put most of my energy into my career and into trying to heal, mentally, emotionally and spiritually. I never completely overcame that deep sense of loss, but eventually I began to believe that I was healthy enough to be reunited with my son.

When I was forty-three, I began my search for my son by hiring a search agency to find him. I began preparing myself emotionally by seeing a counselor who specialized in working with women who had found their adopted children. The counselor also helped me with my other emotional problems.

On August 10, 1992, I had to have my dog put to sleep. As I walked home from the vet's office in tears, I said to God, "The only thing that could possibly make me happy today is some news about my son."

I opened my front door, and the phone was ringing. They had found out who he was! That was when I heard my son's name for the first time—and his last name was almost the same as the first name I had given him! I wrote

Evie

"Kevin Richardson" in bright blue letters on a piece of paper and hung it on the wall. "This is real," I kept saying to myself. "This is really happening."

The agency promised to send me a copy of his birth certificate and said they'd soon have his telephone number. Holding his birth certificate in my hands, it was so strange to see all those statistics that belonged to the two of us—date of birth, time, weight, my doctor's name—but with someone else's names listed as parents. And there I was, crying again. It was hard to believe that I still had tears of grief, considering how much counseling and crying I had already been through.

I had to keep reminding myself that I placed him for adoption because it was best for everyone concerned. I do believe that, but it never completely took the pain away. I hung his birth certificate on the wall next to his name and just tried to absorb it all.

About a week later the agency called again to say they didn't know where he was yet, but he had an invalid California drivers license from a few years ago. They told me he was six feet two inches, 185 pounds, had brown hair and green eyes. They told me to be patient. It would be any day now. Each new piece of information I received about him helped me get ready for him. It was very similar to the long labor I had experienced twenty-four years before.

I met with an adoption social worker who had dealt with other birth-mother-child reunions, and read some books to help prepare myself. She suggested I write a letter to my son, including all the important things I wanted to say, just in case he didn't want to meet me. I wrote the letter, but I couldn't think about him not wanting to meet me. I wanted to have the deepest kind of relationship a mother could have with her child!

The morning of October 30, about four months after my initial contact with the agency, they informed me that my son was living in Nebraska. I rehearsed what I would say over and over. The whole day I could think of nothing but that phone call. I decided not to call that day, but to wait until the next, which was Saturday.

I couldn't sleep that night. All my fears about being rejected surfaced, and I lay there in the dark, wondering if I was doing the right thing.

I tried meditating to calm my mind and my fears. I kept thinking, "By the end of this day, I will have talked to my son, something about which I have

133

dreamed for twenty-four years!" For almost an hour I dialed his number and hung up before it rang. Would he hate me? Would he be angry with me? Would he just hang up and I'd never get to talk to him? Finally, I let it ring. A young woman answered. I asked for Kevin. She said he was at the grocery store and would be back in half an hour. I told her I'd call back. I paced. I cried. I called my friends, my mom, my brother. I thought I was going to hyperventilate, I was so nervous. I called back.

I said, "Is this Kevin Richardson?"

He said, "Yes."

I said, "Were you born November 24, 1968, in San Francisco, California?"

"Yes, I was."

"Are you adopted?"

"Yes, I am." As the agency had suggested, I then asked him if this was an okay time for him to take a very personal phone call. He told me it depended on what I had to say. I took a deep breath.

"This is Evie Bennett. I live in Minneapolis, Minnesota. Kevin, I believe I am your birth mother."

There was a long pause and he said, "I've been waiting for this call all my life. What took you so long? Is this really my mom? Are you really my mom?" We talked for almost an hour then and spoke to each other every day for the next month.

When I confided in him that I had been afraid that he might have been angry with me for placing him for adoption, he said, "I always figured that it wasn't a good time in your life to raise a baby and that you loved me so much that you gave me to my mom and dad. Did it happen any other way?"

I told him that was exactly how it was. He suggested that we meet in person—and soon.

He wondered what I was doing for Thanksgiving and would it be okay if he and his girlfriend Maggie drove up and stayed for a few days.

The days and weeks leading up to Thanksgiving were wonderful. We talked almost every day and started discovering similarities. We both used the same slang expressions, we were both allergic to milk, we both had big ears

Evie and her birth son

while growing up. He wears his hair short on the sides and a pony tail in the back—just like how I wear my hair.

During one conversation, he mentioned that his favorite smell was cocoa butter. Cocoa butter! I told him about talking to him while rubbing cocoa butter on my pregnant tummy. We were both amazed.

The first picture he sent me I took immediately to the photo store where I had eighty copies made to include in the "Birth Announcements" I sent out to just about everyone I knew. I was overjoyed!

But by the time Kevin and Maggie arrived at my front door, I was a nervous wreck. I hugged Maggie, but my son and I could only stare at each other. Finally, I gave him a quick hug and said, "Hi."

"Hi," he answered. We talked about unimportant subjects like movies and the weather. But I couldn't keep my eyes off him. I wanted to take off his shoes and socks to count his toes, just like any new mother, but I had to remind myself that this wouldn't be appropriate.

I wanted to hold him in my arms, tell him a story, rock him to sleep, watch him breathe—everything I didn't get to do before. We stayed up late that night, talking and laughing. We couldn't get enough of each other.

He told me all about his childhood and his family. His life sounded so happy and healthy. Then he came over to me and held me, as if he were the parent and I the child. "Thanks for letting me be here," he said.

My counselor had told me that we would go through a period where our bodies would crave each other. She said my body remembered giving him up and his body has a memory of being given up. She said that for a while, until we felt secure that we wouldn't lose each other again, our bodies would need plenty of reassurance.

I don't know if I can describe the feelings I experienced the first time he called me mom. That was one of the regrets I had had since my hysterectomy—that no one would ever call me mom. The feeling of being someone's mom was so powerful. That Thanksgiving season was the happiest of my life. It was the first time I could wish him "happy birthday" in addition to sharing Thanksgiving dinner with him at my table with the rest of my family.

Meeting my son has changed everything about my life. The secret hole inside is finally filled up—with the love of my son. We reassure each other that both of us are here to stay. I feel an inner confidence that I never felt before. I'm sure I did the right thing in giving him up, though. I know I would have been an overprotective, nervous mother. I would have smothered him.

I know I wasn't cut out to be a full-time mom, but I'm awfully lucky to be able to be a part-time mom. Life is finally okay—in fact, I'm excited about life. We talk on the phone several times a week and see each other every few months. He is talking about moving to this area to go to school and to live with me, or at least near me.

We are so close. I always knew we were, but at the same time, I couldn't have dreamed that it would be this good. Having Kevin in my life has even helped heal my relationship with his biological father. The two of them are getting to know each other now.

My family has accepted Kevin completely. My relationships with men have changed because I'm no longer looking to take care of them. I can be a woman with men now, rather than a mother.

Evie

My depression has healed since meeting Kevin. I enjoy my life now. I even enjoy working because it's fun to work hard, knowing I can buy things for my son and spoil him rotten!

My mother is happy to have Kevin in her life. My sisters and brothers knew about him for years before I found him and shared my excitement and anticipation. My father is still drinking, and I've chosen to stay away from him. He did meet Kevin once, though.

When Kevin met my mom, sisters, and brothers for the first time he said, "I feel more connected to those people than I ever felt to my own family."

Kevin's family has been wonderful about the whole thing. The first time I met them they said, "Thank you for our son. We love him very much." I think his mother is somewhat bothered by our relationship, though. She doesn't want to talk to Kevin about it. On the other hand, Kevin and I talk about everything—we have become so close.

He has a good relationship with his adopted father, and I am so grateful for that. When I went to their house, his father brought out a photo album of Kevin when he was little. What a cute child! A little later, his mother left the room, came back and handed me a book. It was Kevin's baby book.

It took everything in me not to cry as I slowly read each page. I remembered back to when I was in so much pain about him, and here I was, more than twenty years later, sitting in the home in which he grew up, his baby book on my lap, drinking 7-Up with his parents and finally knowing that everything was fine. No more wondering, no more fear. Just gratitude that he had a good, solid family. And what makes me most grateful of all is that I have my baby back—forever!

* * *

Chapter Ten

ɞ *Jill* ശ

A thousand generations, every one was new—
A thousand generations leading straight to you.
Everyone will tell you that you're just passing through.
Everyone will tell you, everything you do
Sooner or later comes back to haunt you.
(lyrics from the song, "Super-Human")

We were three Jewish girls growing up in a Jewish neighborhood just outside of Detroit, Michigan. Kitty, the eldest, was smart and beautiful. Penny, the youngest, had a slight hip deformity, was much protected and much pampered. I was just Jill, in the middle, never quite as good as Kitty, never quite as beloved as Penny.

Father was a pharmacist, and Mother had been an elementary school teacher until marriage. Mother was diagnosed with multiple sclerosis before I was born. No one ever told me what was wrong with her until I was eleven years old. It was much later that I understood that my mother was extremely angry about being cut off in her prime. I've been told that she'd been very active and intelligent—the life of the party. My mother's anger spilled into every part of our family life. My parents originally planned to have six children. Personally, I'm very glad they didn't.

Since I didn't understand the circumstances of my mother's anger, and since I suffered from what today would probably be called low self-esteem, I just wordlessly assumed that I was bad in some unremarkable way. This I regarded as normal because I never thought anything should be different, or that I deserved better. With a child's incredible ability to accept, I never thought about it at all.

It seemed that other people knew of my mother's illness. When we were attending Penny's graduation from elementary school, one of the teachers introduced us to some other teachers saying, "These are three of the bravest girls I know." My sisters and I were baffled. We never thought of ourselves as brave. We thought of ourselves as undeserving of praise of any kind. We were barely measuring up to what was expected of us, as far as we knew.

Maybe it was because of being brought up in the 1950s, but I was taught that I had no feelings worth mentioning. My confidences to my mother were often exposed; my shortcomings discussed with others. If I felt sad and talked about it, I was told I'd get over it. I began writing poetry in sixth grade (doesn't everybody?) in an effort to try to understand my world.

Kitty and I formed a close bond because we both identified our common enemy as Mother. We didn't really connect with Penny, who was four years younger than I and seven years younger than Kitty. My mother told Kitty and me about menstruation in a matter-of-fact way. I never asked about anything else. Kitty and I compared notes and pieced together the rest of the "facts of life" for ourselves.

> . . . My mama told me when I was a child
> "Be careful . . . don't you get too wild—
> 'Cause those who are different—
> They just never fit in . . ."
> (lyrics from the song, "Unconventional")

I remember grade school as a cookie-cutter operation, stressing sameness and not rocking the boat. I received fairly decent grades but certainly didn't achieve what I could have. I always loved music and began piano lessons at the age of four. It was later discovered that I have what is called perfect pitch. My musical talents and singing voice earned me some praise by my teachers, rescuing me from the oblivion I might otherwise have experienced.

I felt close to my father, but he was mostly absent. Although he never discussed finances, I think he had to work long hours to make ends meet, due to the expense of my mother's illness. I loved the few nights a week when he was home. Then we had real dinners like a real family. The rest of the time everybody ate on the run.

I believe my parents truly loved each other when they got married, but my father couldn't adjust to my mother's illness. He never really dealt with her emotional changes. By illustration, years after my mother's death in 1984, my aunt asked at a family gathering, "Was your mother angry?"

My sisters and I all said, "Yes," and my dad said, "No," at exactly the same moment. He stood there, staring at us in astonishment.

Being a pharmacist, my father had access to new ideas about treating my mother's disease. One time he tried tranquilizers. She must have liked the effects because she ended up addicted to them. It's hard to say whether she degenerated because of her illness or her addiction. Or maybe it was a combination of the two. After a while, my father started being home less and less. She eventually noticed, and they started fighting often.

Kitty and I were teens by then, and even more of my mother's rage was turned on us. Although we were fairly normal, obnoxious teenagers, Mother's reactions were beyond normal. When we complained to Dad, he suggested we "bite our tongues" rather than talk back, which of course made no difference at all. Mother would still rage.

In 1960, during my thirteenth summer, I got involved with a Zionist Youth Group. This was part of a back-to-Israel movement that was very strong at that time. The leaders of the group convinced my parents to let me go away to camp for two whole weeks! The site was a beautiful state park setting at the top of Lake Michigan's lower peninsula at the meeting of two Great Lakes.

It was the first time I had ever been away from my family. Everything seemed so peaceful and fun. I played my guitar and sang for the others—my first real audience! I was heartbroken when it was over. My mother was afraid I'd get "the Zionist bug" and move to Israel and they'd never see me again. What I did get out of my Zionist adventure was the resolve to get away from Mother at the first possible opportunity, and try to keep peace until then.

Jill

In high school, I was given some kind of an academic ability test, in which I scored in the ninety-eighth percentile or above in most areas. This resulted in an almost standing appointment with the guidance counselor, who continued to point out to me how I wasn't even close to my potential. I guess it was also standard procedure then to require students like me to meet with a psychologist. At those meetings I was completely uncommunicative. I doubt if I could have articulated how I felt, and my attitude was, "what difference would it make, anyway?"

I was quite shy around my classmates and was self-conscious about my very crooked teeth. I was relieved when my parents finally allowed me to get braces. When the braces came off, I came out of my shell. Until that point my friends were mostly other Jewish girls from the neighborhood. Now I started having friends who were boys. It was intoxicating! I might have even had fun if I'd had any confidence, but I had no faith in my own feelings and wanted the boys' approval desperately. These were flirty little relationships—nothing serious. But I started feeling like I had found a road to freedom. My mother, as usual, was furious. Our fights became more and more intense.

> . . . I wanna be
> Unconventional—Out of the ordinary—very
> Unconventional—One of a kind
> Unconventional—Totally individual
> Unconventional—One of a kind . . .
>
> (lyrics from the song, "Unconventional")

Around the age of sixteen, I got bored with my circle of friends. It seemed like all they ever talked about was clothes, boys, and make-up. I started being friendly with a more serious and mature group of kids. I had an admirable teacher at that time, too, who began to groom me for college. My closest friend in school, Lorna, encouraged me to take difficult courses and was very supportive. "I know you can do it," she used to tell me.

Lorna had been adopted by a Jewish family. We had both been raised to believe that Jewish girls always did the right thing. Therefore, sex before marriage was unthinkable, as were babies before marriage. This was in the 1960s, and "getting a reputation" or having a child out of wedlock was considered the absolute worst thing that could happen to a girl. I know how irrational this is now, but we all believed it then. I remember asking Lorna once about her birth mother. "Do you think she was Jewish?" "Of course not!" Lorna retorted. "Jewish girls don't have illegitimate babies!"

After a series of major screaming matches with my parents, my older sister moved away from home. She never told my parents her address or phone number. I was the only one who knew where she was, and I knew that she wasn't telling me everything. It wasn't very long before I heard a rumor that Kitty was pregnant. My own sister! I couldn't believe it at first because I admired her so much. But it was true. She made the best of the situation, though, and got married. Eventually she re-established relations with Mother and Dad.

Jill

I moved out of my parents' house in January 1965, three days after my eighteenth birthday. I had a job that paid fifty-five dollars a week and I bought a 1957 Ford for two hundred fifty dollars. I told my parents I wanted to go to a nearby community college. They didn't like it, but I was eighteen—and free! I found an apartment for seventy-five dollars a month and rendered it spotless in fifteen minutes flat. That's how small my place was. It was hard to make ends meet, but I was completely happy.

My girlfriends were green with envy. The guys were very interested, and I was very naive. I had allowed myself to be talked out of my virginity the year before by my then-boyfriend. Horribly guilty about it, I thought I could negate my action by never doing that again. I had definitely been awakened sexually, though, and as it turned out, my expectations for myself were unrealistic.

Jill

One night at the Pizza Palace, I met Jeff. He was so smooth and good look-ing—it was like there was an electric current between us. I was quite smitten with him at first. He was very intelligent and evidently his parents had plenty of money. It seemed inevitable that we would become sexually involved.

I think I let having my own apartment fool me into believing I was ready for all sorts of "adult" behavior. One night our sex was unprotected. The next day, I remember counting the days since my last period on the calendar over and over again. It was exactly fourteen days, and I had always been regular. I was filled with dread and, as it turned out, not without cause.

When I became absolutely sure, I told Jeff I was pregnant. I said I didn't want to marry him. I didn't want any trouble with his parents or mine, and I wasn't going to ask him for money.

I felt so angry! What I mostly wanted was for him to go far, far away and let me deal with it. He lived up to my expectations to the letter. He went far, far away, without a murmur—except to ask me if I was sure it was his. The last time I saw him before that conversation, he had fallen asleep, drunk, with a cigarette in his hand, and set his mattress on fire.

It was pretty clear that he was an alcoholic and had other problems, too. I've never been sorry I didn't marry him.

> . . . So how do you know which one it is?
> One thing's for sure—it ain't in his kiss.
> How do you know? How do you tell them apart?
> Until I'm certain, I'll just hold on to my heart . . .
> (lyrics from the song, "Bad Love")

My anger turned into denial, and I kept up that internal fiasco until I got my first case of morning sickness. Reluctantly, I realized I was going to have to make some decisions. I couldn't raise a child on fifty-five dollars a week and had no prospects of financial security.

Trying to raise a child under my circumstances would be grossly unfair to the child. Although there were rumors in my school of girls who had given up babies, single parents were almost unheard of then. Even divorced mothers were stigmatized—and so were their children. I thought that surely there must

143

be a couple somewhere who could give my baby a decent life. I knew what I had to do, but I didn't know how to do it. And I did not want my parents involved. I was very, very frightened inside, but I knew I had to keep my head.

That's what I did for the whole nine months—completely buried my emotions in order to get through it. Because of our strained relationship, my usual routine was to call my parents only a couple of times a year. Perfect. I moved in with another woman and left no forwarding address, so no one I knew could find me until it was all over.

My parents never knew I was pregnant; nor did my younger sister, who was only fifteen and couldn't be trusted. Kitty was the only member of the family who knew. My older sister was to keep that deep dark secret for twenty-four years.

I'm still grateful to my friend Lorna, who was emotionally supportive to me. As often as I could, I visited her in East Lansing, where she was attending college. She had a boyfriend that her parents totally opposed. Our both being in the midst of family rebellions cemented our already close relationship. Lorna was the only one of my old friends with whom I remained in contact. Eventually, she ended up marrying that boyfriend and having five children with him.

Around the middle of my pregnancy, I remember starting to worry about what I was doing with my feelings. "What if I can't get back in?" I thought. "What if I'll never be able to feel emotion again?" But I knew I couldn't afford to spend time worrying about it because being "outside" my emotions was the only way I could survive.

One day when I was walking out of my apartment, a woman who lived down the hall started talking to me. I don't know how she knew, because I wasn't showing yet, but she flat out asked, "Is there a little one on the way?"

After I confirmed her suspicions, she told me about her little daughter, one year old then, who was growing up back home in Tennessee, believing her grandmother was her mother.

The woman, Ellen, was in a lot of pain. She recognized the buried pain inside me immediately. In fact, she invited me to live with her rent-free until the baby came. I could pay her back later. Her apartment was just a little larger than mine, but Ellen and I managed well for the next four months.

Jill

The people for whom I worked found out I was pregnant and fired me. The office manager was kind enough to give me the name of a temporary employment agency run by a friend of his. I accepted a position as an office assistant for a bustling ad agency. I went to work every day in multiple girdles and big clothes. Luckily, I didn't show very much. Even at eight months.

Perhaps the most ironic thing that happened during my pregnancy was meeting Len, the man who lived next door to Ellen. We became very close, but I wouldn't let him be involved with my pregnancy. In fact, I hid the fact that I was in labor the night my contractions started. Years later Len and I would marry and divorce, but we would always remain friends.

The hospital in which my child would be born was just across the street. My doctor lived in an apartment upstairs. Ellen helped me find a lawyer who would handle the adoption. This sort of blind luck had followed me through my whole pregnancy. Well, they do say that God looks after the children and the fools!

The day before my daughter was born I woke up knowing I was in labor, even though the doctor had said it would be at least two more weeks. I spent most of the day alone. Ellen came home from work about 6:00 P.M., and Len stopped by that evening. We stayed up talking until about 11:00 P.M. Every time I had a contraction I left the room. I just didn't want him connected to this in any way.

Len eventually left, and then Ellen and I crossed the street to the hospital. It took some convincing for the nurses to believe I was in labor, since my stomach was so small. They admitted me finally and told Ellen to go home. I was alone, worried and scared. In spite of it all, I kept my head and kept myself under control.

The baby was born early the next morning. They whisked her away immediately. All I could see was one little blue arm. When I demanded information, the doctor assured me that she was fine and healthy.

I was relieved, but all I could think about was how mad that lawyer was going to be, now that he had to hurry up and find an adoptive couple. I didn't want him to pick someone in a rush.

I had read somewhere that if mother/child bonding doesn't take place immediately, it wouldn't happen at all. Letting myself feel some need to bond with my child, I asked Ellen to walk with me to the nursery. They had positioned my baby with her back to the window as if something was wrong with her. I panicked and asked the nurse to turn her around. The nurse just looked at me and shook her head slowly.

I went back to my room and cried. It was as if all the tears I had buried came pouring out. I knew then that there was something terribly wrong with me.

The lawyer visited my hospital room later that day. I guess I looked pretty pathetic. I've always been small in stature, and I must have looked like Little Orphan Annie. Anyway, the lawyer said that he felt like he had to help me.

He told me about a nice Jewish couple in New Jersey who had been married a long time and had plenty of money. He said he knew them and trusted them. It sounded all right to me. We told the hospital that I was going to keep my daughter after all, and that they should bring her to me.

By this time the baby's father, Jeff, was just a distant memory. Imagine my surprise when I saw my daughter for the first time—and she looked just like him in miniature! I picked her up and held her, working hard to convince myself that I was only baby sitting, and soon I would give her back to her real mother. "Oh, what a cute baby," I thought to myself. Before I left, I tucked away the little hospital document with her hand and footprints, date and time of birth, and the name I gave her, Joanna Ruth Silverberg.

My lawyer flew us to New Jersey, where he acted as my legal guardian. I thought, "I'll just sign the papers and leave." But it wasn't that simple. New Jersey law required an oral statement of intentions before signing relinquishment papers. Furthermore, I was required to not only meet the adoptive parents, but to physically hand Joanna over to them!

I didn't know how I could get through all of that. My stomach was in knots the whole time. The couple seemed years older than I was and very respectable. I gave them my daughter and flew back to Michigan alone.

Back at the apartment, my grief exploded in gut-twisting sobs. I've never cried so hard in my life, and I've never been so bereaved. Just writing about it now, I still feel the shadow of that awful aching loss. Knowing I did the right thing was absolutely no consolation.

Jill

... And the world turns 'round, and the rivers roll,
And I feel you in my body and in my soul.
No matter what I say,
No matter what I do—
I know I'll never be free of you . . .
        (lyrics from the song, "Just Can't Leave Your Love")

Almost right away, I went to work for the temporary agency again, wanting to get out on my own and pay Ellen back. Len and I started getting romantically involved. He was very sweet to me, and I knew I could trust him because he'd seen me at my worst and still wanted me. We were both pretty young—I was twenty and he was almost twenty-one.

Aside from my feelings about Len, I was pretty numb emotionally, although I didn't realize it at the time. I had no real direction. I thought vaguely about getting married, having children and just sinking into some kind of oblivion.

One afternoon the lawyer called to tell me it was time to file the adoption papers. During our meeting I looked across his desk and read my daughter's new name upside down. It had been changed from the name I gave her, but the adoptive couple used her name, Joanna, as the middle name. I was very touched by that. I signed the papers and walked home in a kind of haze.

Len's job required that he move to New York City. I moved there too, and we got married after about a year. I still wasn't thinking much about the future, except that maybe I could have a child soon, to make up for the daughter I couldn't raise.

Wondering about Joanna's whereabouts, I called information and asked for the town in New Jersey where I knew the parents lived. The operator gave me the number, but I never called. I did, however, call information often enough to know the adoptive family lived there for three more years. Then, one day I called, and they were no longer listed.

Len and I began growing away from each other at an incredible pace. Both of us hated our marriage, even though we still liked one another. We agreed to part but we didn't want the stigma of being divorced.

According to New York law if both parties had agreed to have children and one party reneged, the marriage could be annulled. Truth is, I just didn't get pregnant. But that was a good way to end our marriage.

147

After a brief affair with a law student, I began feeling so rejected that I lost interest in everything. I developed an eating disorder and gained thirty pounds in one month! I remember telling Kitty, my sister, that I thought I must not deserve anything good, after what I had done. She did her best to convince me otherwise, but she was having her own problems at that time. Her husband was physically abusive to her and chased after other women. As much as I loved her it was hard for me to believe that either one of us deserved better.

> . . . Bad love will abandon you and then you're better off.
> Bad love is worse than no love at all,
> Bad love is worse than no love at all . . .
>   (lyrics from the song, "Bad Love")

I left New York in 1971, when I was twenty-four, in an attempt to get away from everything. I dusted off my musical skills, became my own version of a hippie and was anxious to travel. I had overcome my eating disorder and pulled myself together once again. I had an idea of going to California to perform. I stopped in Austin, Texas, on the way.

I got a job, entered college and got a B.A. in music and another in anthropology from the University of Texas. I became serious about my career as a singer/songwriter around this time. I performed in Nashville for six months, then in Los Angeles for about five years, achieving some success along the way. I always returned to Austin, though.

By the time I was thirty, I despaired of ever having a committed relationship or children. I started seeing Mick, who attended virtually all of my shows in the Austin area. I knew it would not last but my biological clock was ticking. I allowed myself to become pregnant, knowing that I would be raising this child alone.

Roxanne, my second daughter, was born in 1979. I was joyful. I felt like my whole life had been leading up to her birth. I was so grateful to be able to bring her home.

I had always saved my first daughter's hospital document. Cradling Roxanne in my arms, I held the document in front of her and said, "Roxanne, this is your sister." A friend came to visit just then. She found me with Roxanne on one arm, the document in the other hand and crying.

Jill

Another friend of mine, who knew other women who had lost children the way I lost Joanna, started an informal support group at that time. I didn't know it then, but that was the beginning of Austin's most active adoptive search organization.

Throughout all of this, I never told my family about my first daughter. My older sister and I stopped talking about it, and anyone would think I had forgotten about it. But every year on Joanna's birthday I would wonder where she was, and especially if she was still alive. I couldn't stand the anxiety of thinking about it very long. One year on her birthday I dated everything the next day, and didn't realize until later what I had done.

Sometimes when I held Roxanne's hand and the hand of one of her friends I would think, "This is what it is like to have two daughters."

Once I went to the library to learn how to search for Joanna. I sent a letter to an organization in Michigan and another to New Jersey, explaining the particulars of my first daughter's birth. Michigan sent back a questionnaire, which I completed, but I never heard from New Jersey. In the end I didn't do anything else, because I didn't think I had the right to search.

I married Brian in 1983 when Roxanne was four. What a mistake! It was stormy almost from the beginning. He had a terrible temper, and sometimes I felt afraid. Four years later, I thought things had calmed down. Then Roxanne told me Brian had molested her. He had done it during the night, while I was asleep. I pressed charges, filed for divorce and left him immediately. I have never seen or spoken to him again.

> . . . . But when you look in the mirror
> I know what you see.
> You see yourself waiting
> To be set free . . .
> (lyrics from "Super-Human")

Knowing there were "demons" lurking within me, I began seeing a therapist. I learned that I needed to stop damaging myself and could not risk damaging Roxanne any further. I spent the next two years without men, concentrating on my relationship with Roxie.

Although I told my therapist about Joanna, I never told Roxanne about her sister because I didn't want to burden her with my grief and unanswered questions. When my mother died in 1984, I worked through some of my issues with the therapist, but much still remains unresolved.

In 1987, I won a regional song writing contest, which resulted in my attending a class entitled, "How to Make a Record." Allen, the owner of a small production company, was teaching the class. Interestingly, we traveled in the same circles but somehow had never met. Allen ended up producing my first album—and a whole lot more. He's still my producer/engineer, as well as my beloved. They say the third time's a charm, and it certainly has been for me.

Allen is a wonderful person who also had much from which to heal. When we met he was recovering from a nasty custody battle over his daughter, Marissa. He asked me, "Do you think a person can ever really recover?"

I told him about my first daughter then, and said, "No, I don't think we recover, exactly, but we learn to go on."

> . . . I know it isn't easy to smile,
> When nothing goes the way that you plan.
> But baby, we've got love enough to last quite awhile,
> So if there's rocky roads ahead
> We can walk them hand in hand . . .
> (lyrics from the song, "Years in the Future")

We married two years later. The wedding took place just after Roxanne's bat mitzvah, and my dad and sisters came to Austin for that occasion. It was a full house, but everybody got along, thankfully!

One month after my marriage to Allen, on Christmas Eve, my younger sister Penny called. She said, "Jill, a woman called here for you . . ."

Immediately, I knew. Allen walked into the room at that exact moment and I blurted out, "My daughter's looking for me!"

I heard Penny gasp, "It's true, then?" but the lump in my throat was too big for me to answer her.

Jill

I finally told her it was. She said that some "search volunteer" had called, and then had put Rebecca (my Joanna) on the phone. Penny didn't know whether she was really my daughter or what my response would be.

"I have been waiting for twenty-four years for this moment," I told Penny. Then I apologized for never telling her. Penny told me that Rebecca's adoptive mother had died seven years before, and her Aunt Sally had put an inquiry on the Internet, after finding the hospital bill in the mother's safety deposit box with my name and Michigan address on it.

The search volunteer saw the inquiry and called Rebecca, offering to help her find me. Despite all the bouncing around the country I had done, it took my first daughter only four days to find me. My sister gave me Rebecca's phone number in New York. It was more than an hour before I could decide what to say.

"Rebecca? This is Jill," was what I finally said. I was so nervous I could hardly talk. I could tell she was nervous, too.

I told Rebecca that I had hoped to hear from her when she was eighteen, and then when that didn't happen, I thought maybe at twenty-one, but that didn't happen, either. I told her that I didn't think I should search because I didn't want to disrupt her life. Also, I wouldn't have been able to stand it if I had found out she was dead.

She said that her adoptive mother and father had divorced when she was eleven and that she had been so angry that she ended up in therapy. It was the therapist who told her, without permission, that she was adopted. She became estranged from both her adoptive parents. The mother died when Rebecca was nineteen and she felt too guilty to search for me then, because of the negative relationships with her parents. She felt it would be disloyal to them.

She made one earlier attempt to find me but her adoptive dad mistakenly told her that her middle name had been my first name. Of course, this was before they found the hospital bill in the safety deposit box. If her adoptive mother hadn't died she might never had found me. You see, the mother had not even wanted Rebecca to know she was adopted!

It wasn't until after Rebecca's marriage and the birth of her son, Chad, that she decided there were too many unanswered questions in her life. That was when she asked her Aunt Sally to inquire on the Internet.

Jill's birth daughter and her husband

I called my home number after completing that first conversation with Rebecca. My father answered the phone. He said, "I've been told. Is it true?"

"Yes."

There was a long pause. "So what does this mean?"

I knew that if I didn't make him laugh, at least one of us would have a stroke. "Well," I replied, "for one thing it means you're a great-grampa. I bet you thought you were just a good one!"

It worked, thank goodness. Dad has been wonderful ever since. He even set up a trust fund for my little grandson, Chad. The only reference Dad ever made to my secret pregnancy was that he understood the circumstances but was sad that I had to go through all of that alone.

Rebecca and I wrote letters back and forth, sent pictures and made hundreds of long distance phone calls until the following April when we finally met in person, and I was finally able to hug her and my five-month-old grandson. I can't even describe those incredible feelings. She was so beautiful! And that sweet baby! Rebecca's husband John was in the army so that meeting took place later.

> . . . You look like an angel, you look like an angel—
> And all the time between . . . gone!
> Just like a dream,
> For dreams are like the wind . . .
> (lyrics from the song, "Angel")

We had a little "coming out" party for Rebecca. My dad came out to Austin to meet her, and they hit it off right away. My sisters welcomed her warmly.

Jill

Roxanne was ecstatic to find out that she had an older sister. In fact, she laughed out loud when I told her. "It sounds more like a soap opera than real life," she said.

The only person who seemed negative was Rebecca's adoptive grandmother, who is apparently afraid that I'm going to "steal" Rebecca away from them. My eldest daughter, however, has an enormous heart, and no one is in danger of losing her.

As it turned out, Roxanne needed some adjustment time. My marriage, followed quickly by a new sister, brother-in-law, and nephew was a little much to take at first. But Roxanne and Rebecca are becoming good friends.

When Rebecca and John had their second son, Jake, I went out to New York for a week, to help and to attend the *bris* along with most of her family. Everyone was very cordial, and treated me like a distant relative, which is how I view them. Rebecca introduced me to some of her friends as her "mom." I looked around quickly to see if that offended anyone. If it did, I never knew.

At one point, Rebecca told me that she felt sorry for her adoptive brother and sister because she had a mom and they didn't. I told her to let them know they were welcome at my house anytime. Her brother e-mails messages to me regularly, and we all exchange cards and letters.

From what Rebecca told me, it's obvious that things would have been different if her adoptive mother had lived. Her Aunt Sally confirmed this and said that her mother would have been opposed to her finding me. Perhaps her mother and I might have gotten past the negative feelings, or perhaps not. I don't think our reunion would have gone as smoothly if my mother had been alive, either.

Rebecca and I have talked about our similar issues and feelings about our mothers. I think Rebecca is closer to resolving her problems than I am. But we continue to support and help each other.

I once hesitantly admitted to her that I was afraid I had profited at someone else's expense. She answered, "I think that wherever our respective mothers are now, they understand." I take this as evidence of what a special person Rebecca is.

So much has changed since the reunion. I had always discounted my younger sister Penny as someone not worth knowing, but I found out that she is a delightful human being. In spite of living far apart, she, Kitty, and I are closer than we've ever been.

I knew my dad, in his own way, had been trying to make amends since my mother's death. I had mostly ignored these attempts, but after meeting Rebecca, I was somehow able to let my anger toward Dad go. The barriers dropped away. I found myself more willing to understand his point of view after I gave up the secrets. He's been a champ, too, immediately making a place in his heart for Rebecca and her family.

Allen and Rebecca's husband, John, have gone fishing together and get along just fine. Allen was very supportive to me all through the upheavals that Rebecca's return brought forth. All that sudden surfacing of old memories! He was unbelievably tolerant through it all.

Our lives are as settled as they'll ever be, probably. Marissa, Allen's daughter, lives mostly with us now. She's almost nine years old, loves animals and has beautiful Mexican-American features like her mother.

Roxanne is facing some fairly normal growing up challenges, but we're being consistent with our "tough love," and I know life will work out for her.

My musical career is going smoothly. My first CD has been produced, I perform regularly at various venues around Austin and have even "taken the show on the road."

The newness of my first daughter may have worn off, but not the delight, relief, and gratitude. I never realized how wounded I was until the wound was healed. I am deeply thankful for my daughter being returned to me.

I know that we have been very fortunate. There were lots of other possible outcomes. Nevertheless, even if our relationships had not turned out so well, I believe that the universe was out of balance while we were kept away from one another.

I regret that I couldn't raise Rebecca and couldn't know her. I couldn't know if she had what she needed, or even if she was alive. This still seems wrong to me. I used to have nightmares about the terrible things that could have happened to her. I was never sure if I hadn't just "thrown her to the wolves."

One might relinquish one's rights to parenthood, but one never really relinquishes the child. The universe is back in balance now.

* * *

Linda Back McKay is a writer, poet, creative director, and advertising copywriter whose poems are often created on motorcycle rides. Her work has appeared widely in magazines and literary publications in the United States and Canada. She is the recipient of a residency fellowship from the Anderson Center of Interdisciplinary Studies. Her poems and chapbooks have received a variety of awards. She is the author of the poetry chapbook, *Those Girls Are Always Dancing* (1996, White Space Press). McKay conducts creative writing and poetry workshops in the Midwest. Her full-length poetry collection, *Jazz,* and children's book, *No Kitties!* currently await publication. This is her first nonfiction book. She lives with David McKay in South Minneapolis. They have helped each other raise four wonderful children and treasure every moment with her birth son and his family.

Judith Connor